Translation and Literature in East Asia

Translation and Literature in East Asia: Between Visibility and Invisibility explores the issues involved in translation between Chinese, Japanese and Korean, as well as from these languages into European languages, with an eye to comparing the cultures of translation within East Asia and tracking some of their complex interrelationships.

This book reasserts the need for a paradigm shift in translation theory that looks beyond European languages and furthers existing work in this field by encompassing a wider range of literature and scholarship in East Asia.

Translation and Literature in East Asia brings together material dedicated to the theory and practice of translation between and from East Asian languages for the first time.

Jieun Kiaer is an associate professor in Korean Language and Linguistics at the University of Oxford, UK.

Jennifer Guest is an associate professor in Japanese at the University of Oxford, UK.

Xiaofan Amy Li is a lecturer in Comparative Literature at the University of Kent, UK.

Routledge Studies in East Asian Translation
Series Editors: Jieun Kiaer
University of Oxford, UK
Xiaofan Amy Li
University of Kent, UK

Routledge Studies in East Asian Translation aims to discuss issues and challenges involved in translation between Chinese, Japanese and Korean as well as from these languages into European languages with an eye to comparing the cultures of translation within East Asia and tracking some of their complex interrelationships.

Most translation theories are built on translation between European languages, with only few exceptions. However, this Eurocentric view on language and translation can be seriously limited in explaining the translation of non-European literature and scholarship, especially when it comes to translating languages outside the Indo-European family that have radically different script forms and grammatical categories, and may also be embedded in very different writing traditions and cultures. This series considers possible paradigm shifts in translation theory, arguing that translation theory and practice need to go beyond European languages and encompass a wider range of literature and scholarship.

Translingual Words
An East Asian Lexical Encounter with English
Jieun Kiaer

Translation and Literature in East Asia
Between Visibility and Invisibility
Jieun Kiaer, Jennifer Guest, and Xiaofan Amy Li

For more information about this series, please visit: www.routledge.com/languages/series/RSEAT

Translation and Literature in East Asia
Between Visibility and Invisibility

Jieun Kiaer, Jennifer Guest, and Xiaofan Amy Li

LONDON AND NEW YORK

First published 2019
by Routledge
2 Park Square, Milton Park, Abingdon, Oxon OX14 4RN

and by Routledge
605 Third Avenue, New York, NY 10017

First issued in paperback 2022

Routledge is an imprint of the Taylor & Francis Group, an informa business

© 2019 Jieun Kiaer, Jennifer Guest, and Xiaofan Amy Li

The right of Jieun Kiaer, Jennifer Guest, and Xiaofan Amy Li to be identified as authors of this work has been asserted by them in accordance with sections 77 and 78 of the Copyright, Designs and Patents Act 1988.

All rights reserved. No part of this book may be reprinted or reproduced or utilised in any form or by any electronic, mechanical, or other means, now known or hereafter invented, including photocopying and recording, or in any information storage or retrieval system, without permission in writing from the publishers.

Trademark notice: Product or corporate names may be trademarks or registered trademarks, and are used only for identification and explanation without intent to infringe.

Publisher's Note
The publisher has gone to great lengths to ensure the quality of this reprint but points out that some imperfections in the original copies may be apparent.

British Library Cataloguing-in-Publication Data
A catalogue record for this book is available from the British Library

Library of Congress Cataloging-in-Publication Data
Names: Kiaer, Jieun, author. | Guest, Jennifer, author. | Li, Xiaofan Amy, author.
Title: Translation and literature in East Asia : between visibility and invisibility / Jieun Kiaer, Jennifer Guest, and Xiaofan Amy Li.
Description: New York, NY : Routledge, [2019] | Series: Routledge studies in East Asian translation | Includes bibliographical references and index.
Identifiers: LCCN 2019003360 (print) | LCCN 2019005839 (ebook) | ISBN 9781351108669 (pdf) | ISBN 9781351108645 (mobi) | ISBN 9781351108652 (epub) | ISBN 9780815358275 (hardback : alk. paper) | ISBN 9781351108676 (ebook)
Subjects: LCSH: Translating and interpreting—East Asia. | Chinese language—Translating—East Asia. | Japanese language—Translating—East Asia. | Korean language—Translating—East Asia.
Classification: LCC P306.8.E18 (ebook) | LCC P306.8.E18 K53 2019 (print) | DDC 418/.02095—dc23
LC record available at https://lccn.loc.gov/2019003360

ISBN 13: 978-0-815-35827-5 (hbk)
ISBN 13: 978-1-03-240152-2 (pbk)
ISBN 13: 978-1-351-10867-6 (ebk)

DOI: 10.4324/9781351108676

Typeset in Times New Roman
by Apex CoVantage, LLC

Contents

Acknowledgements vi

Introduction 1

1 Making classical Chinese literature contemporary: translation 'between centre and absence' 13
XIAOFAN AMY LI

2 Layered translations: glossing, adaptation and the reception of Bai Juyi's poetry in premodern Japan 49
JENNIFER GUEST

3 Translating invisibility: the case of Korean-English literary translation 81
JIEUN KIAER

Index 118

Acknowledgements

This book emerges from a collaborative effort among the three co-authors, who thank each other for their lively discussion, detailed comments on each other's drafts and collaborative work. Moreover, this research would not have been possible without the generous funding support of the John Fell Fund and the National Library of Korea, which allowed us to host a workshop on translation in East Asia (September 2017) that provided some crucial ideas for this book. We are also grateful to all of the workshop participants for their thought-provoking presentations and discussion.

Jennifer Guest

I would like to thank my other colleagues, friends and family who have generously talked over this project with me, particularly Kōno Kimiko, Nan Ma Hartmann and David Lurie. Professor Kōno was kind enough to host me at Waseda University for a term of research leave while I was working on this project, and I greatly appreciated the chance to attend her seminars and chat with her about questions of premodern textual culture; while at Waseda, I also led a discussion-oriented public workshop on the topic of translation and premodern Japan and benefited tremendously from the thoughtful comments and observations of the participants.

Jieun Kiaer

I am thankful for all the participants in the workshop on translation in East Asia (2017), especially Matthew Reynolds for his insightful comments on multilingualism in translation. Among others who participated in my translation seminar courses over the years, Ben Cagan, Sophie Bowman, Derek Driggs, Anna Yates-Lu, Yeogeun Kim and Karolina Watroba in particular gave me the inspiration and motivation for my chapter.

Xiaofan Amy Li

I am grateful to colleagues with whom I have held extensive discussions about translation and Chinese literature, especially Matthew Reynolds, Lucas Klein and Yang Fu, whose comments have offered much insight into the topic of this book.

I would also like to thank the Chiang Ching-Kuo Foundation/European Association for Chinese Studies travel fund for its support of my library trip to Cambridge to check sinological materials, including key editions and translations of the *Zhuangzi* that formed the essential materials for my book section on translating classical Chinese literature. Simultaneously, I also extend my thanks to the EACS committee members for considering my funding application, especially Bernhard Fuehrer.

Introduction

This book arises from some shared concerns about the relations between translation and literature in three East Asian cultures, namely, China, Japan and Korea. These concerns are, first, how translation engages with multilingualism in East Asia past and present, raising in particular the question of translation between different layers of high-register literary language and between written and spoken vernaculars; second, the Chinese script and classical Chinese canonical texts as a shared linguistic and textual heritage in both premodern and modern East Asia, which provides comparative and interconnecting contexts of literary circulation, translation and reception; and third, various reading, writing and commentarial practices in East Asia that may be considered translational in different degrees and ways and how they offer new food for thought about the concept and theories of translation. Our angle of approach to these common concerns focuses on one specific question that runs through them as a connecting thread: the question of visibility and invisibility in relation to translation.

Since Venuti's *The Translator's Invisibility* (1995), invisibility has been a focus of critique in translation studies. Whether it involves the invisibility of the translator as playing a co-creative rather than subservient role in relation to the original text or the invisibility of translation through domesticating the foreign to produce a smooth, highly readable and marketable end product, translational invisibility has been criticised for being less ethical and aesthetically interesting than visibility. Later critics such as Spivak (2005), Booth (2008) and Coldiron (2012) have generally established a critical consensus in translation studies that emphasises making visible the foreign as a more ethical approach to the cultural Other (especially non-Western source texts). Invisibility is therefore correlated with neutrality, insignificance and effacement, whereas visibility carries positive connotations of increasing translational awareness, linguistic experimentation and the ethics of signalling alterity. Nevertheless, these arguments about invisibility and visibility in translation are almost exclusively based on translation between

Anglo-European and non-Western literatures and have mainly focussed on a specific set of issues: the invisibility or domestication of foreignness, the invisibility of the translator and her creativity and the visibility of the Other. We believe that there are other issues pertinent to thinking about translational (in)visibility as well as other types of invisibility and visibility. One recent theoretical intervention into translational invisibility takes the phenomenological view of invisibility as the 'plus-value' of objects' visibility, e.g., Scott's (2012: 62) suggestion that the original text's invisibility is a 'latent multi-perspectivalism' that translators and readers 'can never properly achieve'. In this way, invisibility is not only inevitable in translation but sometimes even enriching for readers' experience. This shows that all has not been said about (in)visibility, especially in the East Asian context. To explore new insights on this issue we ask questions such as: Is invisibility always a negative aspect for translation and translators? And is visibility always positive? What is rendered visible or invisible by translating East Asian literatures, particularly when translating between East Asian languages and their different varieties? Why is it important for the mediation of translation and the translator's role to be visible to readers? How and when is something made visible through translation, perhaps at the cost of obscuring something else? (In)Visible to whom and made (in)visible by whom, for what purposes and in what contexts? Maybe it is precisely the understanding of invisibility that needs to be diversified and made more visible in discussions about translation, rather than easily dismissing invisibility as undesirable.

The preceding questions are examined in more detail in three chapters, each treating a particular case study focussing on China, Japan and Korea. In the Chinese context, we may first briefly consider Chinese terminology and concepts about translation to see if they refer to invisibility and visibility. The most straightforward and commonly used modern term for translation, 翻譯 *fanyi*, carries various connotations of significant movement, explanation and re-organisation. 翻 *fan* denotes 'reverse', 'repeatedly study', 'rearrange', 'multiply', 'contradict' or 'fly'; whereas 譯 *yi* was sometimes used interchangeably with 擇 *ze* 'select' and 異 *yi* 'different', 'foreign', as well as to denote 'transmission' (傳 *chuan*), 'replacing languages' and 'explain'. Compared to 'translation', etymologically meaning 'carrying across' and suggesting transferring the same thing in one direction from one context to another, the connotations of *fanyi* emphasise making changes in multiple directions and re-organising materials. Going back in time, premodern Chinese terms for translational activities are extremely varied, ranging from early Chinese mentions of 達 *da* ('make accessible'), 寄 *ji* ('entrust', 'transmit'), 象 *xiang* ('likeness-rendering') and 譯 *yi*, mentioned in the 禮記 *Book of Rites* for interpreting officers who communicated with foreign tribes, to terms for interpreters 象胥 *xiangxu* ('likeness-rendering officers') in the 周禮 *Rites of Zhou*, 舌人 *sheren* ('tongue people') in 國語 *Guoyu* (fifth to fourth century BCE), 度語 *duyu* ('word measurer (conversing interpreter)') and 筆受 *bishou* ('translator-scribe') in the medieval collaborative translation activities of Buddhist texts.[1] Notably, the use of 象 *xiang* conveys the idea of visual resemblance, and the notions of 達 *da* ('getting [the meaning] across') and 信 *xin* ('sincere', 'trustworthy') have featured prominently in Chinese theoretical discussions of translational principles.[2] These Chinese terms and notions about translation, however, do not directly relate to the question of (in)visibility. In Chinese scholarship on translation, translational (in)visibility has also been scarcely discussed, with the exception of a few post-2000 Chinese articles that mostly respond to Venuti. Nor are the ideas of making visible the original text via foreign elements in the translated text and asserting the translator's importance given much attention by Chinese translators and translation theorists.

Nevertheless, the fact that (in)visibility has not been extensively discussed in translation in the Chinese context does not mean that it is not a potentially important question. In fact, relating (in)visibility to translation and literature in China shows several significant issues that have been hitherto relatively unremarked. Firstly, intralingual translation between different forms of Chinese languages is so far an unduly neglected topic, since both Chinese and non-Chinese scholarship in translation studies have focussed on translation between Chinese and other obviously non-Sinitic languages, especially English. Secondly, translation across time – especially how translating classical Chinese literature into modern standard written Chinese involves different interpretive practices and problems compared to translating modern and contemporary Chinese literature into English – needs to be brought to the foreground of our attention. These two issues thus relate to two kinds of (in)visibilities, which are the focus of Chapter 1 on 'Making classical Chinese literature contemporary': the visibility of discontinuities and inter-connections between different Sinitic languages, particularly the high literary and lower written vernacular forms and their historical changes, and the invisible relation between traditional commentary (注疏 *zhushu*) and modern Chinese translation of classical texts. Addressing these two (in)visibilities, Chapter 1 argues that it is through translation that the distance between classical and modern Chinese languages and the changing nature of textual production in China over time are shown or obscured. It is of course a truism to say what is called 'Chinese' is an umbrella term for diverse Sinitic languages that have existed in a diglossic condition separating written and spoken forms since the late Han (25–220 CE) and that major groups of spoken forms, such as Mandarin, Wu and Min, are mutually unintelligible and more appropriately called 'topolects' rather than 'dialects'

(Mair 1991: 4). But this truism has been paid little attention in translation studies concerning Chinese literature and deserves more examination in specific case studies.

In particular, the term 'classical Chinese' is especially confusing because it gives the false impression that it is an old form of the same Chinese language that evolved continuously into modern standard written Chinese. Strictly speaking, classical Chinese, also known as 古文 *guwen* 'writing of antiquity', denotes the written language of foundational early Chinese texts, such as the Confucian classics and Masters texts (子書) from the late Zhou (c. 770 BCE) to the end of the Han (220 CE). Post-Han literary Chinese, though loosely also considered classical Chinese, is, however, an 'imitation' (Dong 2014: 80) of classical Chinese writing from 770 BCE to 220 CE, seen as the high literary form to emulate. Modern standard written Chinese, in contrast, is an artificially invented written vernacular based on spoken Beijingese. It emerged from the 白話 *baihua* movement in the early twentieth century and was institutionalised through language reforms from 1956–58 that simplified Chinese characters, defined the *pinyin* romanisation system, and firmly established the use of punctuation. Intralingual translation of classical Chinese literature into modern Chinese for twentieth-century and contemporary readers therefore offers an exemplary case showing how translation can render visible or invisible linguistic, cultural and historical differences underlying the interpretation, circulation and reception of Chinese literature. For example, one notable aspect about translating classical Chinese literature into a living modern form of Chinese is that this type of translation itself is a very recent phenomenon. The first modern Chinese translation of the 道德經 *Daodejing* was in 1956, followed by the 莊子 *Zhuangzi*'s and 論語 *Analects*'s translations from the 1970s-80s. Since the 1980s, many more modern Chinese translations of early Chinese texts have emerged and proliferated. Before the twentieth century, instead of translations, there was a rich and accumulating tradition of Chinese commentaries for classical texts. Given the difficulty and antiquity of these texts for later readers, whether they are medieval literati or Chinese readers today, why did full translations of these classics into a contemporary vernacular form of Chinese start to be produced only in the twentieth century?[3] Chapter 1 therefore aims to address this question – so far unexamined in existing scholarship – and demonstrate that it says much about translation as a key aspect of the modern Chinese reception and transformation of the past, as well as about the nature of premodern exegetical commentaries in the absence of contemporising translations. Here, the important question of the relation between commentary and translation also emerges. Subsequently, the visibility of the Chinese literatus commentator should be considered comparatively with the translator's visibility.

The preceding questions also confirm that classical Chinese literature not only remains as pertinent to translation in the Chinese context as modern and contemporary Chinese literature but also reveals changes in literary reception and interpretive activities from premodern to modern periods. This is why, in Chapter 1, the chosen case study is the *Zhuangzi* – a classical text (c. fourth to third century BCE) in an exuberant but difficult language that inspired centuries of commentaries and multiple translations. By comparing various translations of the *Zhuangzi* into modern Chinese, modern Japanese, English and French, the chapter shows some specific problems of translating classical Chinese that may contribute to our understanding of processes of translation and of the distance between intralingual and interlingual translation. The chapter ends by arguing for a more diversified and nuanced understanding of translation, besides its most straightforward meaning as transference between two distinct and mutually unintelligible linguistic codes. It also highlights the mutually obscuring and revealing inter-relations between different Sinitic languages, as well as how readerly and commentarial activities engaging with classical Chinese literature changed significantly with the advent of the modern printing industry and Chinese modernity.

Turning to the Japanese case, the history of written literature in Japan is woven through with translation, at least in a broad sense of 'linguistic engagements bridging two substantially different varieties of spoken and/or written language' – yet many of these engagements have limited visibility in modern scholarship because of their imperfect fit with assumptions about national languages and the relationship between writing and speech. Chapter 2 will focus on the diverse reception of classical Chinese poetry in premodern Japan, specifically 白居易 Bai Juyi's 'New Ballads' (新楽府), and rethink how translation might fit into this picture. One key question at stake here is how (or whether) to distinguish translation from forms of basic literacy, in this case logographic reading in which written characters can be linked to words in a target language (Japanese *kundoku*); another key issue is how (or whether) to distinguish translation from other forms of interpretive activity, like commentary or adaptation. Keeping all of these practices provisionally within the same frame, the chapter explores the connections and contrasts that appear within the full spectrum of linguistic and literary negotiations with Bai Juyi's work.

Early Japanese literacy developed as a flexible system that could use Chinese characters both logographically, based on translational equivalences established by early readers and writers (including literate immigrants from the continent), and phonographically, with sound values adapted from a variety of Chinese (Lurie 2011). Early on, Japanese readings tended to remain in the realm of ephemeral spoken language (only indirectly visible from our later viewpoint), but by the tenth century, there was a flourishing culture of written glosses linked to classical Chinese texts. A balance of standardisation and factional differences shaped the evolving collaborative system of translational equivalences used to read classical Chinese and write texts in a similar style. This system also informed the development of mixed-script 'kundoku language' as a written style based on this kind of reading practice, giving rise to replacement translations that made full Japanese versions of classical Chinese stories and poems more transparently visible. Such translations often involved significant adaptation to fit new genre needs – for example, the highly codified use of intertextual keywords to incorporate the essence of a classical Chinese story or poem into a new composition. With many variations in style and practice along the way, the gloss-based approach to translation and its surrounding stylistic ecology of replacement translations continued as an influential model through the late nineteenth century, shaping engagements with European languages and even the discourse of national language reform.

One driving force behind the culture of glossing classical Chinese texts was that the visibility of the 'original' text remained desirable and central to textual culture, even when localised Japanese readings were widespread in practice. This is partly a function of the status attached to the Buddhist sutras and other continental classics that formed the sites of early encounters with literacy, which led classical Chinese to develop as a cosmopolitan language in Sheldon Pollock (2006)'s sense, or a 'dead' (written) language living on in a sacred role in the sense that Jean-Noel Robert (2006) has termed a hierogloss. But the example of classical Chinese poetry, which is my main focus in this case study, suggests additional reasons – the visual form is not 'merely' symbolic but keeps a living importance alongside sound in the presentation of poetic patterns. Structural features of Chinese-style poetry like parallelism, prosodic patterning and end rhyme are linked to a particular ordering of characters, easily disrupted by the syntactic rearrangements of localised reading – so that creating or appreciating texts in these genres is a multilayered process involving both Chinese-style written language and paratextual interpretation. This interpretive layer of gloss-based translational reading is flexible, and depending on the situation might lack a visible written form entirely, be inscribed in a range of more or less marginal paratextual positions or replace the Chinese-style text and circulate in its place. The visibility of local language forms was acceptable or desirable in some styles of writing, while others sought to participate in a wider cosmopolitan culture of writing by keeping traces of local reading invisible or at least marginal.

The particular forms of translation that developed in premodern Japan reflect underlying debates about the visibility of speech – should written language strive to make speech visible or to maintain its own distinct kinds of visual patterning, or is there a way to do both? Glosses appear to make ephemeral spoken readings visible and permanent (though they are not actually doing this in a straightforward way, and they often inscribe other kinds of information as well), while remaining in supplementary positions surrounding the visual patterns of a written text. At a more complex level, commentaries may add layers of explanation and relevant information (including vernacular translations) or even supplant the original text entirely; at times, they do this by calling on personal and speech-based sources of authority, as in the case of medieval commentaries framed as notes on lectures. Many texts and practices seem structured by implicit connections drawn between classical Chinese and writing, on the one hand, and Japanese language and speech on the other – a set of associations that would tend to make translation into Japanese invisible, concealing it in the transition between writing and speech – but there are strong forces pulling against these links as well, as with the calligraphic display of written waka poetry or the importance placed on proper Sino-Japanese (i.e. untranslated) pronunciation and vocal performance in many classical Chinese texts.

Unsurprisingly, the balance of visible and invisible translational activities surrounding classical Chinese poetry varies over time and by social setting – audience is crucial, as are shifts in the roles and identities available to the translator. Particularly prior to the early modern rise of print culture and wider access to vernacular reading, glosses and commentarial explanations were often transmitted as prized cultural capital within educational lineages or shared with valued patrons, making knowledge of particular translational equivalences and techniques the mark of membership in a select scholarly group. Meanwhile, adaptations of Chinese poems into the form of Japanese court poetry (*waka*) or classical Japanese tale literature (*monogatari*) had their own patterns of selective circulation within literary networks. Readers and writers engaging with classical Chinese poems adopted various creative roles, particularly those of the teacher, the poet and the storyteller; the translations they performed were often anonymous or couched in terms of poetic composition, retelling for different audiences or annotation based on learned scholarly standards.

The invisibility of a clear role labelled 'translator' or a single act that can be neatly equated to 'translation' reflects the importance attached to a different range of linguistic and literary distinctions. Premodern Japanese texts could be distinguished in terms of a complex set of mutually entangled but not fully dependent factors – including script (the balance of Chinese characters used logographically or phonographically and of letters from the two *kana* syllabaries), style (choices of vocabulary, grammatical structures and rhetorical features), content, established genre and performance context. This can mean that distinctions like Chinese versus Japanese are rendered invisible, for example when continental forms like *kanshi* (Chinese-style poetry) are composed in an orthodox manner as a sign of membership in a wider cosmopolitan community. It also means that more visibly localised kinds of Japanese language (those termed 'vernacular' in this kind of cosmopolitan/vernacular model) are diverse and structured by their own distinctions, as is illustrated for example with the establishment of *waka* poetry as a local but high-status and 'classical' mode of composition. As a result, thinking about premodern Japanese translation involves considering a broad spectrum of spoken and written styles of language, as well as a variety of practices used to negotiate between them – some of which may look like forms of basic literacy, like methods of interpretive commentary, or like translingual modes of literary composition rather than neatly fitting stereotypes about translation in other cultural contexts. With this in mind, Chapter 2 sets out to trace some of the varied translational activities surrounding Bai Juyi's poetry in premodern Japan, exploring how they might suggest a more flexible and inclusive model of translation.

Translation studies involving East Asia have demonstrated that there is a significant asymmetry between translating East Asian material into English and English material into East Asian languages. In the case of Korean, in particular, countless Western sources were translated into Korean beginning from the start of the twentieth century, predominantly from English. Since then, the English language and the materials written in it have received special attention in South Korea. Despite showing reluctance in opening up their country in the late nineteenth century, since having done so, Koreans have been very quick to absorb everything possible from the West. In particular, they were eager to learn and use English. Consider the following quote from I Chongguk in 1937, an extract from *Modŏn Oeraeŏ Sajŏn*, the first loanword dictionary in Korean. It is surprising that after only about 30 years of being officially open to the West, English words had become so popular in Korean as to have multiple complaints levied against them (underlining added for emphasis):

> I have heard comments from various people moaning that, 'I can't make out what the recent newspapers say because they use too much English'. Indeed, foreign language has been trespassing on our modern society (particularly for the last ten years), so much so for this period to be termed the 'Era of Foreign Language Intrusion'. Every single newspaper and magazine now mixes up foreign languages with Korean. So-called modern writers and artists are competitively adopting foreign language, and sometimes almost thoughtlessly parade it . . . Now the journalists look like they are incapable of writing a single sentence without using foreign words.[4]

(I, C. 1937: 1)

Compared to English-to-Korean translations, the number of Korean-to-English translations is very small and is only now starting to grow, especially following the international success of *Please Look after Mother* (trans. Chi-young Kim, 2011) by Shin Kyung-sook and *The Vegetarian* (trans. Deborah Smith, 2015) by Han Kang.

Chapter 3 will discuss issues that arise in Korean-English literary translation, with a main focus on invisibles – forms and functions that do not exist either in the source texts (ST) and languages (SL) or in the target texts (TT) and languages (TL). Korean and English are linguistically quite different, and encountering invisibles at all linguistic – lexical, syntactic and pragmatic – levels and cultural levels is very common (See Kiaer 2017). Hence, translators working in these two languages may face more difficult challenges than translators who deal with linguistically and culturally similar languages. For instance, as we shall explore, Korean-to-English translators need to create categories such as gender and number and must always determine and elaborate the subject of a sentence. These categories in Korean are usually implied rather than stated, with the author encouraging the audience to find it out from the context. Translators into English need to guide their English-speaking readers by making said invisibles into visibles. Some of these processes are forced onto the translators by linguistic conventions, but others are left to the translator's discretion. For instance, in translating address terms and kinship terms, translators have freedom both in regard to whether to translate them and, if they decide to do so, how to treat them in the target language. In addition, Korean-to-English translators have major challenges in dealing with Korean particles which set interpersonal, emotional context for the text as they have no equivalent place in English.

Translators should not necessarily make all invisible expressions visible in the TT. Translators have freedom in choosing what to make visible. Though there are linguistic requirements and conventions that one has to follow regardless of one's preference, translators can still exercise their freedom as to whether to follow the socio-political conventions of the SL culture. For instance, some Korean-to-English translators may want to preserve the age-sensitive, hierarchical nature that is manifested in Korean in their English translations. Others may want to liberate the English text from such conventions. Chapter 3 will reflect on these questions in more detail and connect them to ways of rethinking mainstream translation theory, which is so far predominantly based upon translation between European languages and does not discuss the previously mentioned hurdles in dealing with invisibles resulting from radical differences within language and culture.

As mentioned, Venuti (1995) discussed the notion of invisibility in the context of the longstanding preference in the Anglophone world for the creation of fluent target texts, with no signs of intervention from the translator (who is expected to be invisible). Venuti criticised this trend of erasing all traces of foreignness as a form of ethnocentric violence, arguing that translators should deliberately foreignise their translations to balance this violence. In agreement with Venuti, Chapter 3 asserts that it is important to recognise the role of the translator. But it also argues for the primacy of the translator's discretion. The translator should be considered the co-author of a new translated text, and the treatment of these invisible expressions is his or her personal prerogative. Moreover, in our multilingual era, where English is playing a role as Lingua Franca (ELF) and people of diverse cultural backgrounds are reading texts in English, the concept of domestication and foreignisation needs to be carefully rethought. This is because English no longer singularly represents any monolithic set of Anglo-American values. The number of English speakers in the world has been growing continuously for many years, and that growth is set to continue into the future as well. Even so, the primary makeup of the English-speaking population is simultaneously going through drastic changes. This is because, although the number of English speakers is increasing, the proportion of speakers for whom English is their first language is actually decreasing. The mechanism behind the increase in numbers of the English speakers is not simple population growth of people who speak English as their first language but rather the explosion of English as a second language. As more and more people learn English as a second language, the existence of many diverse English-speaking communities will continue to challenge the idea of who owns the English language. Just as divergence following population movements has resulted in differences between the Englishes of native speaking groups – such as British and American speakers – so too should we expect differences between the Englishes of communities for whom English is a second language.

The Korean case study in Chapter 3 presents Potts's multi-modal, expressive semantics (Potts 2005) and Halliday and Matthiessen's systematic functional linguistics (Halliday and Matthiessen 1999). While Potts argues for the multi-dimensional nature of meanings, Chapter 3 argues that translators can select and reassemble meanings given by the ST author in order to create new meanings for the translated text. Halliday and Matthiessen emphasise the interpersonal function of languages, but translators are not merely dealing with textual information; they are engaging in activities that are inherently multi-modal, register-sensitive, interactive and dynamic. Accordingly, the gradient model of translation is proposed, wherein the author's meanings and the translator's meanings have essential commonalities but are not the same. The more they share, the more translated work will be considered as relevant (Gutt 2000). However, this is not the ultimate goal of translation. Translators can choose the degree of the shared meanings. By using examples from Korean-to-English literary translations, focussing on kinship/address terms and speech styles, and looking at poetry (where translators' creative potential is most clearly manifested), Chapter 3 maintains that translators are not subordinate to the ST authors but instead are co-creators of the translated target texts.

Conclusion

The challenges of thinking about translation and literature in East Asia as outlined here will, we hope, contribute to thinking about translation theory and expanding its frontiers. Mainstream translation theory, still heavily dependent on intra-European comparisons of language and culture, is seriously limited in explaining the translation of non-European literature and scholarship, especially when it comes to translating languages outside the Indo-European family that have radically different scripts and grammatical categories and are embedded in different conceptual and cultural frameworks that pose fundamental questions about the definition of 'translation'. This book supports an ongoing paradigm shift in translation theory, arguing that translation theory and practice need to go beyond European languages and encompass a wider range of literature and scholarship.

By engaging with specific case studies and broader theoretical aspects of translation, this book should therefore suit both the specialist reader interested in technical aspects of translating East Asian literatures and the reader who seeks to reflect on broader questions of translation not limited to the East Asian context. This book is not a history or overview of literary translation in East Asia, although connections between the premodern and modern will be traced to highlight issues of literary reception and linguistic change reflected by translation. The book's argumentative coherence is not chronologically dependent or concerned with a linear narrative of the evolution of translational activities in East Asia but is thematic and comparative: focussing on what translation renders visible and invisible, on the (in)visibility of translation itself and on the complex network of relations between different linguistic forms; readerly and writerly activities; and circulation and reception of texts across time and space.

Notes

1 Cheung gives a good summary of different Chinese terms for translation in her *Anthology of Chinese Discourse on Translation* (2006).
2 See Cheung (2006), and Yan Fu's preface to 天演論 *Tianyanlun* (1898), where Yan advocates the translational principles of 信 *xin*, 達 *da* and 雅 *ya*, referring to the Buddhist scriptural translator支謙 Zhi Qian's (c. 252) theories.
3 There seems to be no study addressing this question so far. Intralingual translation

from classical to modern Chinese is also poorly recognised as a proper area of examination or serious sinological activity, with only a small number of Chinese articles treating the topic (see Zhang Zaiyi and Liu Weijie 2011), mostly in response to the new wave of modern Chinese translations and cautioning against using translations to replace engagement with the original classical text.

4 '요새 新聞에는 英語가 많아서 도모지 알아볼수가 없다'는 不平비슷한 말을 나는 여러사람의 입에서 흘러나오는 것을 들었다. 實로 現代(더욱 最近 十年以來)는 '外國語闖入時代'란 이름을 붙일만큼 外國語가 闖入하고 있다. 新聞이란 新聞 雜誌란 雜誌는 모두 外來語를 混織한다. 소위 모더니즘의 文人墨客들은 다투어 外國語를 移植하며 때로는 거의 思慮없이 羅列한다. ... 오늘의 쩌널리스트는 外來語를 쓰지않고는 記事한줄 못 쓸 形便이다'.

Bibliography

Booth, Marilyn. 2008. 'Translator v. author (2007)'. *Translation Studies* 1 (2): 197–211.

Cheung, Martha P. Y., ed. 2006. *An Anthology of Chinese Discourse on Translation*. Manchester: St Jerome Publishing.

Coldiron, Anne Elizabeth Banks. 2012. 'Visibility Now: Historicizing Foreign Presences in Translation'. *Translation Studies* 5 (2): 189–200.

Dong Hongyuan. 2014. *A History of the Chinese Language*. London and New York: Routledge.

Gutt, Ernst-August. 2000. *Translation and relevance: cognition and context*. 2nd ed. Manchester: St Jerome Publishing.

Halliday, Michael and Matthiessen, Christian. 1999. *An Introduction to Functional Grammar*. London: Arnold.

I Chongkŭk. 1937. *Motŏn chosŏn oe-rae-ŏ sachŏn* (Modern Korea Loanwords Dictionary). Sŏul: Hansŏng tosŏ chusik hoesa.

Kiaer, Jieun. 2017. *The Routledge Course in Korean Translation*. Abingdon: Routledge.

Lurie, David Barnett. 2011. *Realms of Literacy: Early Japan and the History of Writing*. Cambridge, MA: Harvard University Asia Center.

Mair, Victor. 1991. 'What Is a Chinese "Dialect/Topolect"? Reflections on Some Key Sino-English Linguistic Terms'. *Sino-Platonic Papers* 29.

Pollock, Sheldon I. 2006. *The Language of the Gods in the World of Men: Sanskrit, Culture, and Power in Premodern India*. Berkeley: University of California Press.

Potts, Christopher. 2005. *The Logic of Conventional Implicatures: Oxford Studies in Theoretical Linguistics*. Oxford: Oxford University Press.

Robert, Jean-Noël. 2006. 'Hieroglossia: A Proposal'. *Nanzan Institute for Religion and Culture* Bulletin 30: 25–48.

Scott, Clive. 2012. *Translating the Perception of Text*. Oxford: Legenda.

Spivak, Gayatri. 2005. 'Translating into English'. In *Nation, Language, and the Ethics of Translation*, ed. Sandra Bermann and Michael Wood. Princeton: Princeton University Press, 93–110.

Venuti, Lawrence. 1995/2008. *The Translator's Invisibility*. London and New York: Routledge.

Yan Fu. 1898/2013. 天演論*Tian yan lun*. Shanghai: Shanghai shijie tushu.

1 Making classical Chinese literature contemporary

Translation 'between centre and absence'

Xiaofan Amy Li

Introduction

Although the translation of modern and contemporary Chinese literature – especially into English – has enjoyed a boom after the 1970s, this chapter focuses on the case of translating classical Chinese literature because it not only presents a broader range of translational problems but also draws connections and comparisons between the premodern and modern, between receptions across time as well as across cultures and space.[1] The specific text chosen as an example is the 莊子 *Zhuangzi* (c. fourth to third century BCE), a philosophical and poetic text written mainly in classical Chinese prose (古文 *guwen*), posthumously canonised as one of the four Daoist foundational classics.[2]

The translation of classical Chinese literature not only is a sinological concern for premodern specialists but offers much food for thought on translation in the Chinese context broadly speaking. Firstly, for modern readers, classical Chinese literature needs to be translated not only into languages such as English and German but also into modern Chinese, which raises questions about intralingual translation across time and space. As mentioned in the introduction, classical Chinese is a literary written form that consolidated its style and status in early China and was then artificially maintained as the high variety of written language by Chinese scholarly and courtly elites (later called 文言文 *wenyanwen* rather than *guwen*) until the twentieth century. Translating classical Chinese into modern Chinese – a standardised language based on spoken Mandarin – inevitably involves translating across significant linguistic and historical differences, although both are considered Sinitic languages. Indeed, classical Chinese is remote to the modern reader because of its antiquity and different cultural context, the past being 'a foreign country' (Lowenthal 1985). Intralingual translation between classical and modern Chinese – though so far an understudied topic[3] – can make more visible the questions and constraints of modern translations of ancient texts that grapple with historical differences. Secondly, the history of translating Chinese literature is very much the history of translating *classical* Chinese literature. Besides the exceptional *Daodejing*, translated into Sanskrit as early as the seventh century and eventually becoming the most translated text in the world after the Bible, before the post-war era, Chinese classics were the texts of choice to be translated into English and other European languages.[4] Moreover, before the twentieth century, Chinese classics – especially Confucian and Buddhist canons and premodern poetry – formed a commonly shared textual corpus in the Chinese script world, including Japan, Korea and parts of Southeast Asia, where readers typically read the original Chinese texts with the help of commentaries and reading aids (e.g. Korean *gugyeol* and Japanese *kundoku*) with some translational function.[5] The twentieth-century turn to focus more on modern and contemporary Chinese literature and its English translations should not obscure the fact that classical Chinese literature has been highly visible in pre-twentieth-century East Asia and Southeast Asia and formed a paradigm of literature-in-circulation. Thirdly, the translation of classical Chinese literature reveals important shifts in Chinese literary history. In particular, the changing readership of classical Chinese literature from premodern to modern periods has significantly transformed the landscape of readerly and interpretive practices. Up until the early twentieth century in East Asia, there was an absence of extensive translations of Chinese classics into a language contemporary to their readers; instead, we find the tradition of writing commentaries to explain and present arguments about canonical texts, such as the *Analects* and the *Zhuangzi*, practiced almost exclusively by and for the scholarly elite. After 1950, however, commentarial scholarship declined significantly, whereas full-length modern Chinese and modern Japanese translations of Chinese classics aimed at general readers started to appear. The shift from commentary to translation raises questions about their inter-relation and suggests that modernity in East Asia – not least Chinese modernity – was a fundamentally *self*-translational enterprise, besides being translational and 'translingual' (Liu 1995) towards the West. Rather than repeat the latter truism about Chinese modernity and translation of the West and to some extent Japan, this chapter's discussion shifts the attention to Chinese self-translation, and shows that modern Chinese translations of classical texts are also *modernising* translations, forming one crucial aspect of the modern Chinese reception of antiquity that seeks to re-interpret and contemporise the latter for Chinese readers today.

The *Zhuangzi* and its modern translations provide an incisive perspective on the previously mentioned issues. The reason for choosing the *Zhuangzi* among all the possible classical Chinese texts is not least because it is, besides its philosophical and even religious aspects, an undisputedly *literary* work, befitting this book's focus on literary translation. Moreover, the *Zhuangzi* holds a paradigmatic and exceptional place in Chinese literature, which the Belgian-French poet Henri Michaux's (1936) expression 'entre centre et absence' ('between centre and absence') perfectly captures. Both a canonical text since the Western Han (206 BCE to 9 CE) that amassed a formidable volume of commentaries throughout the centuries *and* a 'persistent form of marginality' (Saussy 2017: 97) due to its eccentric and anti-orthodox ideas, the text has always posed extreme challenges to its commentators and interpreters. Written mostly in late archaic Chinese typical of fourth to third century BCE texts (apart from possible syncretist sections written later than the third century BCE),[6] the *Zhuangzi*'s language is remote enough from modern Chinese to offer a good example of translation across time. Additionally, the text's style is notoriously difficult, abstruse and imaginative, stretching not only the limits of translatability but also of intelligibility itself. Finally, since the late nineteenth century, the *Zhuangzi* has been translated again and again into various languages, particularly into English, modern standard Chinese, French, and Japanese. This rich and diverse translation history offers the possibility for comparisons between different translations that may show what different aspects and understandings of the *Zhuangzi* are revealed and obscured by different translational approaches and constraints.

The following discussion first considers the *Zhuangzi*'s visibility in terms of its global circulation and translation and then comparatively reads several different translations to explore specific translational problems, particularly how intralingual translation into modern Chinese contrasts with interlingual translation into English and French. Reflections on intralingual translation and the distance between classical and modern Chinese lead to an examination of the Chinese commentarial tradition in relation to translation. Special attention will be paid to whether commentaries served a translational function before the age of modern translations and how modern translations differ from traditional commentaries. The chapter ends by arguing that instead of an equivalent transcription of the original text that seeks to reveal the latter, we may think of translation as a practice that reformulates meaning and methods of reading, oscillating between different degrees and dimensions of visibility and invisibility.

The *Zhuangzi*'s visibility: the text, its circulation and translation

As a brief introduction to the *Zhuangzi*, it is one of the pre-Qin Masters-texts (*zishu*) allegedly written by 莊周 Zhuang Zhou, a contemporary of Mencius, after whom the text is named, since 莊子 Zhuangzi literally means 'Master Zhuang'. Little is known about Master Zhuang apart from stories about him in the *Zhuangzi* itself and the Grand Historian 司馬遷 Sima Qian's record of him as an extremely erudite writer from the state of 蒙 Meng.[7] The authorship of the text, however, is multiple and some parts are later additions by Master Zhuang's followers. 郭象 Guo Xiang (252–312), a distinguished scholar in the Six Dynasties, edited the *Zhuangzi* into the form of the text that we know today, reducing the text from its then fifty-two chapters to thirty-three chapters divided in sequence of their perceived authenticity as the 內篇 Inner Chapters (1–7), 外篇 Outer Chapters (8–22) and 雜篇 Miscellaneous Chapters (23–33).[8] Guo expunged parts he considered spurious and rearranged certain sections into new combinations, though we do not know exactly what changes Guo made. Moreover, Guo also wrote the most influential commentary to the *Zhuangzi*, which set the standards for later commentators and entrenched the associations of neo-Daoist concepts, such as 自然 *ziran* 'self-so', with the text. The *Zhuangzi*'s textual history therefore tells us that its authorship is multiple and uncertain, its style is inconsistent, its composition dates over a few centuries and it is a syncretist compilation with possible apocryphal sections. These facts about the text already pose a different set of problems as compared to translating a single-authored book in definite form with precise information about the author and her historical background.

As concerns the *Zhuangzi*'s visibility in terms of its literary status and posthumous influence in China, since the Han, the *Zhuangzi* has been the subject of study and of numerous commentaries; the inspiration for eremitic culture, aesthetic ideas, and literary composition; and the key reference to which premodern Chinese literati as well as contemporary writers repeatedly return.[9] Moreover, the *Zhuangzi* has functioned as an important 'textual sponsor' for translating and reconfiguring foreign literature and ideas into China from the arrival of Buddhism to the introduction of French *poètes maudits*, as Saussy (2017: 96) demonstrates. In recent decades, after Chen Guying's first modern Chinese translation and commentarial edition of the *Zhuangzi* (莊子今注今譯) in 1974, many more modern Chinese translations have appeared. This connects with the fact that since the 1980s when interest in traditional culture revived in China, especially in the background of the 國學熱 'National Studies Craze', there has been much desire to reinterpret ancient Chinese texts and translate them for the general public.[10] In this context, the *Zhuangzi* is promoted as part of China's national literary heritage, and some passages from the text (especially chapter one, 逍遙游 *Xiaoyaoyou*) are included in the national curriculum for secondary schools. Chinese scholars have also undertaken big research and editorial projects – supported by much government funding – on classical Chinese texts, e.g. the 《儒藏》 Confucian Canon project led by Peking University since 2002 and the 《子藏》 Masters-texts Canon initiated in 2010 at East China Normal University, starting with the *Zhuangzi* as its first text for research and editorial work. In brief, the *Zhuangzi* has enjoyed very high visibility as a canonical text of exceptional aesthetic and intellectual value in China both past and present. Paradoxically, nonetheless, the *Zhuangzi* remains an obscure text throughout Chinese history: perused carefully by only a handful of scholars; never 'required reading' for the civil service exams as the Confucian classics were (Childs and Hope 2015: 42); having no concrete influence on Chinese political life (except inspiring the literati's withdrawal from politics); more known about than read; much studied but little understood. As Møllgaard (2007: 12) observes, 'anybody who seriously engages *Zhuangzi* must begin with the claim that *Zhuangzi* is as yet not understood'. This invisibility of the *Zhuangzi* – in clear contrast to the visibility of the Confucian canon that has become representative of the core values of the Chinese tradition – is due not only to its baffling language and general strangeness peppered with monstrous animals, mad and deformed characters, hair-splitting argumentation and surreal topsy-turvy scenarios, but also to its marginal cultural status and being un-usable by power (Billeter 2004). In this way, the *Zhuangzi* has remained paradoxically visible and invisible in China, as a canon of anti-canonicity.

Beyond China in East Asia, the *Zhuangzi* reached premodern Japan and Korea and was read and studied as a Daoist classic by the scholarly classes, who could read and write literary Chinese. The text was introduced into Japan during the fifth to seventh centuries and was read by courtly elite who held discussions and sometimes even court lectures about it (Zhang 2005: 12). 林希逸 Lin Xiyi's (1193–1270?) Buddhist-influenced commentary of the *Zhuangzi* also had much influence on haikai poetry schools, especially Bashō, as Qiu's study (2005) demonstrates. Japanese readership of the Chinese classic was very limited, however, and only until the Edo period (1603–1867) was the *Zhuangzi* circulated more widely outside courtly circles (Kame and Sautreuil 2013: 74). Nevertheless, Japanese commentaries and sinological scholarship on the *Zhuangzi* are substantial and reach back to at least the sixteenth century, as enumerated in detail by Yan Lingfeng (1993). In the past century, full-length translations in modern Japanese have been made by prominent scholars such as Fukunaga Mitsuji (1956), Kanaya Osamu (1971), and Akatsuka Kiyoshi (1974).[11] In Korea, the *Zhuangzi* was known at least since the Koryo period (918–1392) (Pratt and Rutt 2013: 94), often under the title of *Namhwa-jin'gyong*, which refers to the text's honorific title 南華真經 *Nanhua zhenjing*. Although Daoist texts and Daoism were for a long time marginalised in Korea because of the dominant Confucian ideology, the *Zhuangzi* was studied as a philosophical and literary text among intellectual circles. As Jung remarks (in Kohn 2000: 800), 'Choson intellectuals were . . . deeply interested in Lao-Zhuang studies' (i.e., studies of the *Daodejing*, also known as *Laozi*, and *Zhuangzi*). Scholars such as Park Saedang (1629–1703) and Han Wonjin (1682–1751) wrote commentaries for the *Zhuangzi* and discussed its philosophical ideas. Full modern Korean translations also appeared in the twentieth century, e.g., by Kim Tong-song (1963) and Kim Tal-chin (1968). In sum, the *Zhuangzi* has enjoyed high visibility in East Asia, not because it was widely translated (which only started in the post-war era) but because East Asian scholarly circles could read classical Chinese and engaged with canonical Chinese literature in their originals. Simultaneously, having never been a state-sponsored text like Confucian and Buddhist classics, the text has remained highly invisible outside its largely specialist readership. The *Zhuangzi*'s visibility in East Asia is therefore not primarily a *translational* visibility but a *lingua franca*-dependent visibility that is unevenly concentrated though geographically widespread.

Beyond East Asia, special attention should be paid to translations and studies of the *Zhuangzi* in Europe and North America since the late nineteenth century, which have much increased the text's international fame. Unlike in East Asia, translation is a pre-condition for the *Zhuangzi*'s circulation among Anglo-European readers, so we are definitely talking about translational visibility here. The earliest translation of the *Zhuangzi* in Europe was Frederic Balfour's *The Divine Classic of Nan-hua* (1881). Herbert Giles's (1889) and James Legge's (1891) English translations followed quickly, resulting in the Chinese text achieving 'an early place of prominence within the "Victorian invention of Daoism"' (Komjathy 2004: 3), attracting readers such as Oscar Wilde (who reviewed Giles's translation in 1890).[12] Since the early twentieth century, about twenty English translations (both full and selected) have been published, including one version by Martin Palmer et al. (1996) and several remarkable translations made by prominent scholars: Feng Youlan (1931), Burton Watson (1968), Angus Graham (1981), Victor Mair (1994) and Brook Ziporyn (2009).[13] In other European languages, the *Zhuangzi* has been most translated into French and German, besides its Dutch, Italian, Polish, Russian and Spanish translations. A few notable ones to cite are the following: in French, Léon Wieger's *Les Pères du système taoïste* (vol. 3, 1913), Liou Kia-hway (1969) – retranslated into Italian by Laurenti and Leverd (1992), Jean Levi (2006/2010); in German (all selected translations), Martin Buber (1910), Richard Wilhelm (1912) and Hans Stange's 1954 *Tschuang-tse, Dichtung und Weisheit*; and several recent Italian translations by Leonardo Arena (2009), P. Nutrizio (2011) and A. Sabbadini (2012). This huge array of different translations shows that the

Zhuangzi has reached a broader readership beyond the sinological circle. Besides translations, scholarship on the *Zhuangzi* has also increased markedly in the past few decades. Since Wu's (1982) dubbing of Zhuangzi as a 'world philosopher', several monographs and numerous articles in different languages on the *Zhuangzi* are produced each year by international publishers. Currently, the *Zhuangzi* is probably the most discussed text from early China in academic literature and from all kinds of perspectives.[14] However, it has not been as translated or popularised as the *Daodejing* or the *Analects*,[15] and its readership remains mostly within an audience who are already interested in classical Chinese literature or Daoism. The recent boom of Chinese studies in Europe and North America also focuses on modern and contemporary China without raising significantly the visibility and importance of premodern Chinese studies (or 'sinology' in its older sense). Like in East Asia, in Anglophone and European spheres, the *Zhuangzi* also oscillates between its visibility as a foundational Chinese classic and invisibility as a highbrow and specialist work.

This overview of the *Zhuangzi*'s circulation and translation in East Asia and the West shows that a text's visibility in the sense of 'the degree [of] public awareness' (as in the OED) and its prominence can be multiple and uneven. Relating the *Zhuangzi* to translation shows not only how much its translation has increased its circulation and readership but also how, notably in premodern East Asia, it was scarcely translated since translation was neither a pre-condition for its circulation nor needed by readers who could not engage with the original text. This relation between translation and its target audience is an important aspect of the reception of classical Chinese literature and will be examined later. Now the discussion turns to some specific problems in translating the *Zhuangzi* through comparing different translations.

Specific translational problems: a comparative reading of *Zhuangzi* translations

The comparative reading of multiple translations is not only 'important for the study of classical Chinese texts' but also enriches our understanding of the original text as 'potentially plural' (Li 2015b: 128). This is particularly true for the *Zhuangzi*, the different translations of which may show us how, for instance, a modern Chinese translation obscures an aspect that a French translation otherwise highlights and vice versa. The following detailed examination considers several important translations, listed here with brief descriptions. Besides being representative in style and approach, these translations are not limited to the perceived most authentic seven Inner Chapters of the *Zhuangzi*. Since interesting examples for discussion about translation occur across the whole text (including possibly corrupted sections), referring to more complete rather than partial translations is necessary.[16]

The list of translations considered is as follows:

- Chen Guying's 莊子今注今譯 *Zhuangzi jinzhujinyi* (1974/2009 revised edition): the first modern Chinese translation and one of the most successful, includes the original text with a comprehensive collection of different commentaries, printed in traditional Chinese characters;
- Fang Yong's 庄子今译 *Zhuangzi jinyi* (2010): modern Chinese translation, scarce on commentary and targeted at general readers, includes the original text, printed in simplified Chinese characters;
- 興膳宏 Kōzen Hiroshi's modern Japanese translation 莊子 *Sōshi* (2013): based on Fukunaga's 1956 translation and interpretation, emphasises the playfulness and literary quality of the text; includes the original text in traditional Chinese characters, a *kakikudashibun* version[17] and some commentaries;
- Angus C. Graham's *Chuang-tzu: Inner Chapters* (1981/2001 reprint): selective translation into English prioritising the Inner Chapters but including many parts from other chapters; philologically oriented, heavily footnoted and unsuitable for general readers; unique in its rearrangement of the *Zhuangzi* sections according to thematic coherence and Graham's assessment of their authorship;
- Burton Watson's *The Complete Works of Chuang Tzu* (1968): full translation into English and one of the most readable; Watson also referred to Fukunaga's and other Japanese translations while doing his English translation;
- Victor Mair's *Wandering on the Way* (1998): full English translation highlighting the *Zhuangzi*'s creative and playful style;
- Brook Ziporyn's *Zhuangzi: The Essential Writings* (2009): selective English translation including a range of Outer and Miscellaneous Chapters, avoids 'standard renderings' and suggests new interpretations (Van Norden 2009: 148), also has the unique feature of including some (translated) traditional commentaries;
- Liou Kia-Hway's *Tchouang-tseu: Œuvre complète* (1969): the first complete French translation, with extensive endnotes, but sometimes lacking in philological explanation;
- Jean Levi's *Les Œuvres de Maître Tchouang* (2006/2010 revised edition): the second complete French translation, preserves much of the imaginative force but sometimes over-translates (as Billeter comments in the appendices); no footnotes or commentaries;

An initial observation is that all the translators in this list are prominent sinologists and scholars. Though not all *Zhuangzi* translations are by academic translators, the sinologist-translator is the norm. This is also true of translators of classical Chinese literature in general. Besides the specialisation of this particular area of translation, the sinologist-translator also shows a different facet of the translator's visibility. Contrary to the much bemoaned fact that translators are not duly credited for their work (especially in Anglophone publishing), sinologist-translators are well recognised for translating difficult classical Chinese texts such as the *Zhuangzi*. Their names are visibly printed on the book cover, and their translational work is seen as a proof of their philological mastery and scholarly credentials. Chen and Watson, for instance, are known primarily for their translational work of classical Chinese literature. This recognition of sinologist-translators is also due to the fact that the discipline of (Anglo-European) sinology emerged through translation projects and has always been fundamentally linguistically and culturally translational.[18]

Format and presentation

The presentation of the preceding translations also shows important differences. Notably, for modern Chinese and Japanese translations, the original text is included with punctuation added, typically preceding the translation and selected commentaries by premodern scholars. Unlike English and French translations, modern Chinese and Japanese translations do not replace the original text but keep it fully visible, encouraging readers to have a look at it even if they cannot fully understand it. In China, in particular, although translated literature is published without the original text, classical Chinese literature is the exception to this rule. This is even the case for adapted translations of Chinese classics for children, e.g. Cai Zhizhong's comics. Including the original text gives an impression of continuity from the ancient text to its modern translation. This continuity is further emphasised by other aspects, such as the consistent use of one Chinese script throughout (either all traditional or simplified characters), printing the text in vertical columns read from right to left,[19] and including traditional commentaries that follow upon the original text printed in smaller font. Chen's *Zhuangzi* translation, for instance, mimics premodern Chinese book formats in this way, with the modern translation printed in the same small font as the commentaries, so that translation is presented almost as an extension to the commentary, seeming to differ mainly in that the translation explains the original text more comprehensively and in continuously flowing language.

Despite the original text's full visibility, the presentation of modern Chinese translations for classical literature like the *Zhuangzi* nevertheless deliberately obscures certain issues. For instance, the consistent use of one script for the ancient text and its modern translation makes the reader unaware that the Chinese script has undergone much change and that simplifying Chinese characters was a radical twentieth-century reform that sparked much controversy in its time. For example, Fang's *Zhuangzi* translation prints the original text in simplified characters, which de-foreignises the archaicness of the *Zhuangzi* and the historical context of its writing. Punctuation is also added to the original text, not only obscuring the possibilities for different sentence breaks but also the fact that premodern texts were not punctuated since sentence breaks should be worked out by their readers. This way of rendering the remoteness of ancient texts invisible is unique to modern Chinese translations (especially published in mainland China) but naturally inapplicable to Western language translations and not practiced in modern Japanese translations, which print the original text in unsimplified characters, many of which do not exist in Japanese *kanji*.

Translation of chapter titles and names

To start with the particular problems in translation, we may consider chapter titles and names in the *Zhuangzi*. Chapter titles are typically, three-character titles for the Inner chapters, e.g., 逍遙遊 *xiaoyaoyou*, 齊物論 *qiwulun*, and 人間世 *renjianshi*, and two-character titles for Outer and Miscellaneous chapters: e.g., 胠篋 *quqie*, 在宥 *zaiyou*, 則陽 *zeyang*, 讓王 *rangwang*, 說劍 *shuojian*, which are often generated from the first two significant characters in the chapter by later commentators. Personal names are often unusual and similar to nicknames, e.g. 齧缺 Nieque, 王倪 Wangni (2.11); 女偊 Nüyu, 卜梁倚 Buliangyi (6.4); 狂接輿 Kuangjieyu (7.2); 壺子 Huzi (7.5); 婀荷甘 E'hegan and 弇堈[弔] Yangang(diao) (22.7). These chapter titles and names are charged with meaning and often highly symbolic, ambiguous and suggestive. For instance, should we read 齊物/論 *Qiwu-lun* 'Discourse on levelling all things' or 齊/物論 *Qi-wulun* 'Levelling all discourses about things'? Is 卜梁倚 a homophonic pun that, when pronounced in old Chinese, sounds similar to 不兩一 *buliangyi*, 'no-binary-oneness'? There are also rare or now-obsolete characters (e.g. 胠, 弇), and strange combinations of characters that form caricatural names with a humorous touch: e.g. 壺子, literally 'Master Gourd-bottle', for a sage who can physically manifest cosmological changes and perfectly embodies the primordial Dao, similar to the gourd that symbolises undifferentiated chaos, the cosmic egg, and self-sufficiency.[20]

Modern Chinese translations and editions of the *Zhuangzi*, Chen and Fang among others, typically keep chapter titles and personal names as they are without any translation, sometimes with additional commentaries or footnotes discussing their meanings and nuances. Not translating chapter titles and names is also quite common in modern Japanese translations, e.g. Kōzen's and Hara Tomio's (1962) translations, although Kōzen explains what the chapter title means immediately following the title, as an introduction to the main text. For English and French translations, however, the translator is obliged to decide whether, taking a more conservative approach, s/he should romanise i.e. phonetically transcribe chapter titles and personal names, or, taking a more creative approach, translate some or all the titles and names into meaningful terms. Generally, the tendency of various translators from James Legge, Graham and Liou to Ziporyn and Levi is to translate the meaning of chapter titles (unless the titles are personal names) rather than give romanised titles that mean nothing to the reader. For example, Graham's 'Rifling trunks' for 胠篋, Liou's 'Laisser faire et tolérer' for 在宥 and Ziporyn's 'Wandering Far and Unfettered' for 逍遙遊. Levi steps up the interpretation of chapter titles by adding, after his translation of the original title, an alternative title he invents to summarise the chapter's central topic, e.g., 'Tsö-yang ou Des influences miraculeuses' for 則陽; 'Randonnées extatiques ou L'envol du cachalot' (Levi, p.13) for 逍遙遊, where Levi's addition 'L'envol du cachalot' ('Flight of the whale') refers to the opening story about the huge fish Kun that transforms into the huge bird Peng, who flies to the Southern seas. With personal names, however, there is wider divergence between translators. Both Mair and Levi have shown their playful imagination by translating names creatively – in the spirit of the *Zhuangzi* that invents these eccentric and caricatural names: e.g. 婀荷甘 as 'Nénuphar Sucré' (Levi, p. 185), 'Pretty Lilysweet' (Mair, p. 218), and 'Woman Hunchback' (Mair, p. 56) for the sage 女偊 Nüyu, whereas in many Chinese translations the possibility that Nüyu is a woman often goes unmentioned, which is not an insignificant detail because the female is particularly valued in Daoism and sagely Daoist figures are often women (unlike exclusively male Confucian scholars). Liou and Ziporyn, however, generally keep to the neutral but uninformative way of romanising names, whereas Graham alternates between romanisation and meaningful translation (p. 58): 'Gaptooth [齧缺] put a question to Wang Ni [王倪]'.

In sum, modern Chinese and Japanese translations leave more untranslated, partly because it is feasible to not translate these special terms by leaving them in Chinese characters – which are legible and at least partially comprehensible to the modern reader (even though the modern understanding of the same character may be substantially different from its ancient meaning); partly because it is extremely difficult, if not impossible, to translate these terms and names into modern Chinese without taking them apart in such a way that they become impossibly awkward and long, e.g. how could one translate 婀荷甘 or 狂接輿 into modern Chinese names? In contrast, English and French translations – i.e., translations into radically different languages – better clarify the meaning of chapter titles and personal names and render more visible their playful and bizarre tone and various nuances.

Special terms

Special terms used in the *Zhuangzi* are difficult to interpret and translate but cannot be easily circumvented by being left untranslated or romanised. Some of these Zhuangzian terms have become idiomatic expressions in literary Chinese as well as modern Chinese, albeit often in a different sense when compared to their original use. I focus on two representative types of special terminology.

Zhuangzi-*specific terms, or so-called 'untranslatables'*

These are terms that only appear in the *Zhuangzi*, possibly coined by the *Zhuangzi* authors, and are hardly used in other early Chinese texts. Thus, we cannot rely on contemporaneous early Chinese texts to figure out a consensual meaning or conventional use of these terms and only have the *Zhuangzi* as reference point. Sometimes these special terms become posthumously an idiomatic trope or allusion (典故 *diangu*) used only in reference to the *Zhuangzi*. We may consider these terms 'untranslatables' that pose 'limits' to conceptual and cultural 'commensurability' (Apter 2013: 590). Nevertheless, as Li observes (2017: 203), the misleading term 'untranslatable' does not really mean impossible to translate and understand in another language but particularly challenging and '*infelicitous* to translate', especially if these terms need to be explained at length instead of being approximated by a manageable single word or expression.

For example, 弔詭 *diaogui*, literally 弔 *diao*, means 'hanging', 'in suspense', 'condole', and 詭 *gui* means 'weird', 'mysterious', 'swindling', or 'paradoxical'. *Diaogui* appears in a passage where the sage Changwuzi says that everything, including his own words, are a dream:

且有大覺而後知此其大夢也， . . . 予謂女夢，亦夢也。是其言也，其名為弔詭。

(*Zhuangzi* 2.12, my italics)

Burton Watson's translation goes:

> And someday there will be a great awakening when we know that this is all a great dream . . . And when I say you are dreaming, I am dreaming, too. Words like these will be labelled the *Supreme Swindle*.
>
> (my italics for the translation of *diaogui*)

To show how the translation of *diaogui* can differ wildly, compare with Ziporyn's translation (p. 19) for the last sentence '是其言也，其名為弔詭': 'So if you were to "agree" with these words as right, I would name that nothing more than a way of offering condolences for the demise of their strangeness'. The difference lies in whether 是 is taken as a demonstrative pronoun, 'this'/'these', or as a verb, 'affirm'/'agree', and whether 弔 is understood adjectivally or adverbially ('hanging' words, even 'upside down' words), or as a verb: 'mourn', 'condole'. Since the *Zhuangzi* text clearly signals that *diaogui* is a coined term describing 言 by giving the definitional structure '... 也，其名為 ...', 'these words, their name is [*diaogui*]', Ziporyn's translation seems less preferable than Watson's, which is also the consensus among the vast majority of translators and commentators (Liou, Chen, Levi, etc.). Nevertheless, the difficulty of translating *diaogui* remains. For instance, Levi's translation reads well but adds phrases that do not exist in the original text:

> Ce n'est qu'à l'issue du Grand Réveil que nous réaliserons que nous éveillons d'un long sommeil *traversé de cauchemars* ... Et moi qui *vaticine* ainsi sur le rêve, *qui sait si* je ne suis pas tout simplement en train de rêver, *à moins que je ne sois le rêve d'un autre*. Toutes mes paroles sont des énigmes ...
>
> (p. 28–29, italics showing additions)

Levi's rendering has a deliberately Borgesian fictionality (e.g. 'The Circular Ruins') about the infinite regression of dream states (which can be considered 'overtranslation', as Billeter remarks in Levi 2010: 343ff). But the translation of *diaogui* as 'énigmes' feels flat and inadequate. Graham, however, captures the sense of movement in *diao* in his 'a flight into the extraordinary' (p. 60), but the nuances of trickery and mystery in *gui* remain unaddressed. Chen's modern Chinese translation '奇異的言談' ('strange and wondrous discourses' p. 98) only preserves the sense of bizarreness, whereas Fang simply leaves *diaogui* as it is. Perhaps owing to the neologism of *diaogui*, it has survived in the Chinese language as a Zhuangzian idiom[21] – although it is rarely used now and cannot be readily understood – denoting something (usually language) that is bizarre, paradoxical, uncertain, incomprehensible, deceptive, riddle-like and surreal. Being ungraspable itself, *diaogui* has become the very figure of obscurity and ineffability.

The various translations cited here show that for *Zhuangzi*-specific terms like *diaogui*, there is no single comprehensive and faithful translation because the terms themselves stretch the limits of language and our understanding. One might suggest the alternative of leaving terms untranslated, thus using their strangeness to emphasise their unique idiomaticness, though footnotes giving detailed explanation would then be necessary. This technique of preserving special terminology through a phonetic transcription is often practiced in studies of non-European literatures and cultures, e.g., the Persian *ghazal*, *rasa* in Sanskrit, *dao* (道) in Chinese, and *iki* (粋) in Japanese. But there are too many such 'untranslatables' in the *Zhuangzi* to take this approach. Rather than find every translation inadequate or lapse into the simplest but most uninformative phonetic transcription, we may recognise that these 'untranslatables' are in fact infinitely translatable and rich in their potentiality to produce multiple translations. Each translation may then show alternative facets of interpretations that gives a fuller picture of the special term.

Faux amis: terms that keep their form and continue to be used in modern Chinese, but their meanings and nuances are different from their original use in the Zhuangzi

I take the idiomatic expression 朝三暮四 *zhaosanmusi* as an example. It literally means 'three in the morning and four in the evening'. It originates from passage 2.6 about a monkey keeper switching from feeding his monkeys three nuts in the morning and four nuts in the evening to four nuts in the morning and three in the evening. In modern usage, *zhaosanmusi* is an idiom for 'being fickle' (particularly having multiple love affairs) and is a negative epithet used to accuse someone of disloyalty and wishy-washiness. In the *Zhuangzi*, however, it is a positive metaphor for the sage's (analogous to the flexible monkey keeper) capacity to 'walk both paths' (兩行), i.e., balance odds and ends, right and wrong, to settle things in harmony. The immediate connotations of *zhaosanmusi* for the contemporary Chinese reader are completely irrelevant to the *Zhuangzi*, whereas the reader who knows no Chinese can benefit from her ignorance by not having any preconceptions. For modern Chinese translations, therefore, what do translators do to highlight such a faux ami to avoid confusion? Although Chen points out (p. 39) that *zhaosanmusi* in modern Chinese comes from this *Zhuangzi* passage, disappointingly, he ignores the problem of different ancient and modern understandings of the idiom and simply gives a plain translation without further contextualisation (pp. 74–75): '養猴的人 . . . 說: "早上給你們三升而晚上給你們四升"'. The addition of the unit measurement 升 *sheng* (one Chinese litre) is also unexplained. Similarly, Fang translates almost identically ('早上給三升, 晚上給四升', p. 28) and gives no further explanation and contextualisation of *zhaosanmusi*. It is impossible for Chen and Fang to not know the modern meaning of *zhaosanmusi*; therefore, they have simply deemed it unnecessary to draw readers' attention to this faux ami.

There are other notable faux amis originating from the *Zhuangzi*: e.g., 小説 *xiaoshuo*, which is the standard and neutral modern Chinese term for the literary genre of 'fiction'/'novel'. In the *Zhuangzi*, however, it appears to mockingly refer to 'petty gossip' which people fabricate and spread in the hope of becoming famous and gaining some reward (26.3). Take another example, 志怪/誌怪 *zhiguai*, which from the late Han (ca. 200 CE) onwards became a common term denoting the literary genre of 'tales of the strange' or 'anomaly records' featuring ghosts, immortals, monsters, supernatural and bizarre phenomena. In the *Zhuangzi*, *zhiguai* appears in chapter one (1.1) as a phrase meaning 'recording and collecting unusual and wondrous things', referring to someone or some text called 齊諧 *Qixie* that records such things, including the story of the mythical Peng bird who ascends ninety thousand miles into the sky and journeys to the Southern Seas. We may observe that the modern meanings of *xiaoshuo* and *zhiguai* are not completely unrelated to their meanings in the *Zhuangzi*. Indeed, the Zhuangzian uses of these terms can inform us about the conceptual evolution of these terms: up until the twentieth century, when the status of *xiaoshuo* rose phenomenally, there was always something trivial and unimportant about *xiaoshuo* in Chinese literary history, particularly when compared to historiography and poetry, the two supreme genres of writing; and *zhiguai* in the *Zhuangzi*, although not a literary genre, already indicates writing that takes particular interest in wonderful, fantastic and monstrous creatures and things (i.e. the gargantuan Peng bird that was a leviathan fish to start with).

How to translate these faux amis for modern readers is certainly a tricky problem and more so for translations into modern Chinese and even modern Japanese than translations into English, French, German and other languages that are radically different from classical Chinese and do not use the Chinese script. On the one hand, modern Chinese and Japanese (to some extent) have formally preserved these terms as they are, and the translator needs to make the reader aware that the Zhuangzian use of these terms does not conform to modern understandings. On the other hand, these faux amis often show a certain continuity from the Zhuangzian's use to the modern Chinese uses (as with *xiaoshuo* and *zhiguai*), so a modern Chinese translation that completely ignores this connection (e.g. Chen and Fang) obscures the linguistic and conceptual evolution that these faux amis embody. This creates a sort of invisible visibility for these special terms. As for translations into radically different languages, although they automatically avoid the confusion between ancient and modern meanings of faux amis because they cannot preserve the terms formally (e.g., Mair translates *xiaoshuo* as 'petty persuasions' (p270)), they almost always render invisible the idiomaticness and dimension of conceptual evolution and connection (unless they add lengthy footnotes),[22] thus creating an invisible visibility again in the opposite way as Chinese translations do.

Particularly ambiguous passages and possible text corruption

Due to posthumous editing and textual loss, there are instances of textual corruption, possible missing sections and arbitrarily patched-up fragments in the *Zhuangzi*'s text. This means that, apart from deciphering the meaning and intention of the text when it is intact, the translator sometimes needs to supplement information, reconstruct the text where there are suspected corruptions and omissions, speculate upon the original wording and re-punctuate sections, to find the most appropriate interpretation.

For example, is the following possible textual corruption?

是故滑疑之耀，聖人之所圖也。

(2.7)

The problem with this sentence lies in the ambiguity of 圖 *tu*, which can lead to two completely different interpretations. According to commentators like Shi Deqing and Billeter, 圖 should be taken in its conventional sense as a verb to mean 'seek', 'desire', so the sentence would literally mean 'Therefore the radiance of the slimy and doubtful is what the sage seeks'. Kōzen's Japanese translation keeps to this interpretation, remaining faithful to the text as it is transcribed (vol. 1, p. 60): 'かくして暗く定かならぬ光を、聖人は自己のものとしようと図るのである'. According to other commentators who are the majority, including Guo Xiang, Jiang Xichang and Wen Yiduo, 圖 is a textual corruption for its ancient variant 啚 (pronounced *tu* or *bi*), which in turn is a variant for 鄙 *bi*, 'despise', 'discard'. In this case, the sentence would mean 'Therefore the sage despises the glitter of glibness and doubt'. Given the passage in which this sentence appears, particularly the emphasis that the sage uses 明 *ming*, 'illumination', 'clarity' to guide himself/herself, the second interpretation, which proposes textual alteration, seems more suitable, for why would the sage pursue slimy darkness and doubt? This explains why many modern translators have agreed with the second interpretation: e.g., Mair's 'The sage endeavors to get rid of bewildering flamboyance' (p. 18), Levi's 'Le saint se méfie de tout éclat louche et trouble' (p. 24), and Graham, Chen, Fang, and so on. Nevertheless, we may also remember that the Zhuangzian sage is in fact often in a state of confusion and undifferentiation: e.g. 混沌 Hundun, 'Undifferentiation' in chapter 7 who has no sensory organs; in mindlessness and ambiguity: e.g., the personality 象罔 Xiangwang, 'Amorphous' or 'Ignorant Image' in 12.4; and in dark, watery places: e.g., 玄水 *xuanshui*, 'black waters' (22.1), and 北冥 *beiming*, 'the dark Northern Sea' (1.1). Given the typical Zhuangzian penchant for paradox, it is not unthinkable that the sage is simultaneously driftingly dim (滑疑) *and* pristinely illuminated (明). After all, it is the shapeless and ignorant Xiangwang who succeeds in finding the lost Dark Pearl (玄珠, 12.4), not 知 'Knowledge' or 離朱 'Piercing Eyesight'.[23]

Taking account of this, then the interpretation and translation of 圖 as 'seek', without making textual changes, is also plausible.

The question this example raises is: if translators of possible corrupted ancient texts are confronted with expressions and sentences that seem out of place or outlandish, should they question the original text and alter it to find an interpretation that suits them better? In some cases, particularly when the sentence or passage appears to be forcefully inserted (e.g. chapter 6 lines 11–14),[24] or upon comparison of different historical editions, some characters are shown to be lacking or superfluous in a sentence (e.g., notes 14 and 18 in Chen (p. 859) for chapter 30.1), or when the grammar is clearly wrong, such textual alterations are more plausible and may restore the text to a more correct form. In other cases, such as the preceding example, there is nothing clearly amiss in the text, and the character variant is more far-stretched. The decision then comes down to the translator's consideration of various semantic contexts, including, as Vávra points out (2017: 66), 'lexical and syntactic context, the immediate textual context, the edited textual context, and the discursive context'. This consideration not only involves a comparative weighting of the importance of these different contexts – e.g., the overall discursive context may be more important than the immediate textual context – but also differing understandings of what each context means, e.g., 'immediate textual context' is seen by some translators as the sentence and passage in which an expression occurs but by others as the whole chapter where this expression is located and even the entire text of the *Zhuangzi*. Therefore, in the preceding example, for both translators who alter 圖 to 鄙 and those who keep the existing 圖, different decisions about whether the existing text should be changed stem from the same concern about faithfully reflecting the most important and appropriate semantic context. These decisions are, however, often invisible to the reader, although they have very real effects on how the translation reads. Moreover, this means that sometimes changing the existing text achieves higher translational fidelity and that this 'fidelity' is not directed towards a single definite 'original' text, since that is impossible for a syncretist and partially apocryphal text like the *Zhuangzi*.

Style and emotional response

The translational challenges of the *Zhuangzi* also include its different linguistic styles that convey varying emotional responses: ranging from conversations to formal prose and mythic fable-like anecdotes to extremely abstract argumentation. I pick one example of dialogue with particular emotional force:

惠子相梁，莊子往見之。或謂惠子曰：'莊子來，欲代子相。' 於是惠子恐，搜於國中三日三夜。莊子往見之，曰：'南方有鳥，其名為鵷鶵，子知之乎？夫鵷鶵發於南海而飛於北海，非梧桐不

止，非練實不食，非醴泉不飲。於是鴟得腐鼠，鵷鶵過之，仰而視之曰："嚇！"今子欲以子之梁國而嚇我邪？'

(17.12)

Mair's translation goes (164–65):

> When Master Hui[25] [i.e., Zhuangzi's best friend] was serving as the prime minister of Liang, Master Chuang set off to visit him. Somebody said to Master Hui, 'Master Chuang is coming and he wants to replace you as prime minister'. Whereupon Master Hui became afraid and had the kingdom searched for three days and three nights. After Master Chuang arrived, he went to see Master Hui and said, 'In the south there is a bird. Its name is Yellow Phoenix. Have you ever heard of it? It takes off from the Southern Sea and flies to the Northern Sea. It won't stop on any other tree but the kolanut; won't eat anything but bamboo seeds; won't drink anything but sweet spring water. There was once an owl that, having got hold of a putrid rat, looked up at the Yellow Phoenix as it was passing by and shouted "shoo!" Now, sir, do you wish to shoo me away from your kingdom of Liang?'

One certainly cannot miss Zhuangzi's biting sarcasm here, not only because he turns the normal analogical relation between equally valued things upside down by equating a rotten rat with the state of Liang and the erudite and powerful Huizi with a stupid, aggressive bird, but also because of his vivid and humorous way of contrasting Hui's petty-mindedness with his own superior vision (i.e., that of the phoenix). Besides the special nouns, 鵷鶵 *yuanchu*, 鴟 *chi*, and 梧桐 *wutong*, which are difficult to translate without explaining their symbolism,[26] the emotional force in the final sentences requires the translator's attention: the onomatopoeic interjection imitating the owl's hissing and screeching sound (嚇！) and the scornful repetition of 子 ('you') in '今子欲以子之梁國而嚇我邪？', i.e. 'now you want to shoo me away from *that* state of Liang *of yours*?' These important stylistics are not always shown in translation. Mair's translation of 'Now, sir, you . . .' chooses a respectful register, whereas Chen (p. 476) simply leaves terms untranslated (see italics): '貓頭鷹仰起頭來叫喊一聲："嚇！"現在你想用你的梁國來嚇我嗎？', which is particularly confusing because 嚇 in modern Chinese is rarely used as an injection (which was its primary use in classical Chinese) and now means 'to frighten', 'threaten'. Chen's use of the conventional 'you' 你 *ni* in modern Chinese is also quite neutral, since *ni* could be used in both polite and insulting language. Liou's and Levi's translations, in contrast, are emotionally bland and sound too rationalised: e.g., '[Le]hibou . . . lui jeta un cri menaçant. N'as-tu pas cherché comme le hibou à protéger ton poste en voulant m'effrayer?' (Levi, p. 142). Kōzen's translation, however, is more emotionally dramatic: Zhuangzi addresses Huizi by 君 *kimi* (vol. 2, p. 351), a 'you' suggesting intimacy and seniority on Zhuangzi's side – which is not factually true since Huizi is both older and higher in social hierarchy than Zhuangzi but appropriate in this passage where Zhuangzi is asserting his superiority over Huizi. Kōzen also translates the neutral 視 'see' in the original text '仰而視之' as にらみつけ (vol. 2, p. 351) 'stare', 'glare', adding more hostility to the owl's screech. What the Japanese translation can do to change the emotional nuances (through different pronouns for 'you' that show intimacy, informality or formal respect), the English translation cannot do, and therefore, the linguistic register inevitably varies across different translations.

There are other tensions underlying this passage using vivid analogy and language that only the cultural context of early Chinese rhetoric and disputation can bring into full force, not to mention an understanding of social hierarchy and friendship at Zhuangzi and Huizi's time. After all, Zhuangzi, who holds no political office, is fiercely criticising the powerful Huizi, even though they are close friends. What was his tone and facial expression when speaking? – Maybe some disappointment besides the sarcasm, i.e., 'as my friend, Huizi, shouldn't you know better'? What would Huizi's reaction to Zhuangzi's criticism be – shame, anger, rebuttal, amusement, relief? Finally, how shocking does this story sound to its author's contemporary audience? What might be obvious or at least easier for the author's contemporary readers to understand and infer is remote and concealed for readers today, who are vastly estranged from both classical Chinese and early China. Translators of such passages therefore need to exercise their imagination to grasp the underlying tensions and emotions in the depicted situation.

The preceding comparative discussion clarifies a few points about translational invisibilities and visibilities in the *Zhuangzi*. Firstly, translating ancient and syncretist Chinese texts like the *Zhuangzi* is often a reconstructive, strongly interpretive and imaginative practice. By altering and reimagining the original text, the binary between the single original text and multiple translations breaks down (which is already a truism in translation studies). More significantly, this translational process does not mean the original text is not important, rather that it is not limited to an externally given and definite form and can be partially formulated by the translator. Moreover, translators still adhere to notions of translational fidelity and philological accuracy and are not creative in the sense of inventing something that takes no account of the original text's historicity. Without referring to the original text, however, often there is no way for readers to know what decisions are made in the translational process, which then remain invisible inevitably rather than be deliberately obscured through some translational ideology about 'fluency' or 'domestication' (Venuti 1995). Secondly, the comparison between different translations brings out more forcefully questions about cross-temporal and intralingual translation. Whether it is the emotional force of language, Zhuangzian neologisms or faux amis, the historical and linguistic contingency of contemporary readers is highlighted to different degrees by translating the ancient text. In particular, precisely because modern Chinese (and modern Japanese to an extent) formally preserve many characters and terms used in classical Chinese, it is more difficult to differentiate between ancient and contemporary meanings and nuances whereas they are typically better clarified in English and French translations. Nevertheless, Western language translations also obscure the terminological continuity and conceptual history inherent in Chinese idioms used both past and present. This suggests that translation between East Asian languages (more similar languages) is weaker and less intervening than translation from classical Chinese or any East Asian language to radically different languages like English and French. Although more elements of the original text are visually displayed (i.e. visible) in modern Chinese translations, this in fact sometimes makes the foreignness of classical Chinese to modern readers less *noticeable* (i.e. more invisible).

The invisibilities shown by intralingual translation from classical Chinese to modern standard Chinese confirm that there is no seamless continuity between the two but a wide distance that is often unnoticed or downplayed. Besides being 'divorced from spoken language for no less than two millennia' and 'a language that may [have . . .] lived only partially in the mouths of priests, seers, and bards' (Mair 1998: iv), classical Chinese differs from modern Chinese in a wide range of aspects such as grammar, vocabulary, logical features, rhetorical construction, discursive context and style. Linguistic studies by Pulleyblank (1995), Harbsmeier (2012), Zádrapa (2011) and Peyraube (2016) have demonstrated many important grammatical points in classical Chinese that differ from modern Chinese, e.g. subjectlessness, monosyllabic vocabulary, the absence of measure words, word-class flexibility. The pronunciation of old Chinese (c. thirteenth century BCE to third century CE, including late archaic Chinese in which the Masters-texts like the *Zhuangzi* are written) is also uncertain and has been the subject of speculative and complex reconstructions, constituting a highly specialised area known as Old Chinese phonology.[27] We still know little for certain about the pronunciation of old Chinese, although it possibly was toneless before 500 BCE and definitely sounds very different from modern Mandarin. In addition to these linguistic and historical differences, the extremely condensed elliptic style and frequent intertextual allusions in classical Chinese texts like the *Zhuangzi* multiply their difficulty, which means that they are indeed very far removed from Chinese readers today, who need some mediating explanation to make sense of these ancient texts. Modern Chinese translations, therefore, meet this need for mediating explanation, which is also necessarily a translation across time where translation *is* the meaning, as Jakobson (1959/2004) asserts. In extension, for an ancient 'book language' like classical Chinese, translation *is* understanding, for nobody can understand it without undergoing a translational process (in the way that monolingual native speakers can understand their mother tongue).

Given the huge historical and linguistic gap that separates classical Chinese literature from Chinese readers today, it is all the more intriguing that the translation of classical texts into modern Chinese is under-appreciated among Chinese speakers and ill recognised as a subject of study in the Chinese-speaking scholarly community. This may be partially due to the fact that, for centuries and even today in China, translation has never been paid much attention unless it is translation of a *perceived distinctly foreign* language. As Alleton observes (2004: 36), since the earliest imperial times, state-sponsored language standardisation efforts have tried to unify 'Chinese space' through a single written language, so that any 'inter-Chinese' translation is not perceived as translation proper. The widespread and enduring belief that Chinese characters serve as vehicle for linguistic continuity and cultural unity – despite the simplification of characters in mainland China that further distances modern Chinese writing from the traditional script – further downplays the difference between classical Chinese and modern Sinitic languages. Chou (2007), for example, argues for the strong continuity from ancient to modern Sinitic languages and asserts that modern Chinese is the best language to teach classical Chinese, re-iterating Yuanren Zhao's (1980) views about teaching classical Chinese like a living language and reading it aloud in standard Mandarin. Although recitation is a long-established practice in the instruction of classical Chinese literature and we can only read ancient texts aloud in a modern spoken language, Chou's and Zhao's views gloss over the separation of literary Chinese and spoken vernaculars and the fact that spoken Mandarin is phonetically very different from classical Chinese. Certain other scholars who better recognise the immense distance between classical and modern Chinese tend to, however, argue against modern Chinese translations because they often contain mistakes and misleadingly vague expressions. For instance, Liu (2011: 67) argues that translating classical Chinese into modern Chinese should be an exercise for 'self-learning' only, not to be published for other readers; the prominent indologist and translator Ji Xianlin also famously expressed the view that '古文今译是毁灭中华文化的方式，必须读原文，加注释即可' 'modern translations of classical texts are the way to destroy Chinese culture, people must read the original text, referring to traditional commentaries would suffice' (2009).[28] This argument for reading classical texts with their commentaries, without relying on translations, is itself very revealing because, firstly, it implies that commentaries can better explain classical texts to contemporary readers than modern translations; and secondly, it in fact points to another important reason for the under-recognition of modern translations: the fact that before the 1950s, classical Chinese texts were never fully translated and instead, commentaries served as the mediating explanation.

What, therefore, are commentaries, if they are not only superior to translations (or are they?) but also function as a substitute for the latter? And what explains the existence of the commentarial tradition instead of full translations for classical Chinese texts before the twentieth century? Many later premodern readers of early Chinese literature, such as the *Zhuangzi*, would, as modern readers today, also find the texts remote, but no translations emerged to fill this hermeneutic gap and commentaries sufficed. Simultaneously, we also observe that the rise of modern Chinese translations in the past century went hand in hand with the substantial decline of the commentarial tradition. Do these imply that commentary and translation are in fact very similar and even share the same hermeneutic function, and therefore one's gains means the other's loss? But if commentary and translation are interchangeable, or if commentary is a superior hermeneutic method, why did modern Chinese translations emerge in the first place, and why do Chinese scholars today not continue writing commentary as their premodern predecessors did? To answer these questions we need to consider the relation between commentary and translation.

Commentary and translation: an invisible relation

To start with, we may briefly consider commentary in the Chinese context by addressing the following questions: What is commentary's style and format? Its purpose and function? Who writes it, and who reads it?

Considering the origins of commentarial practice in early China, as Puett demonstrates (2017), literary production and commentary intertwined via strategies of citing and rereading earlier texts and were in fact co-emergent with each other. Many early Chinese texts 'were in part commentaries to earlier materials, and were in turn shaped into what we have come to know as texts by the commentarial tradition' (Puett 2017: 113). Towards the end of the Western Han, however, the categories of the Masters-texts and Five Confucian classics emerged, which also set the task of later scholars as understanding and explicating these texts of antiquity (古書 *gushu*) by earlier sages, rather than trying to compete with or even supersede them.[29] The kind of commentary as a practice of textual exegesis clarifying earlier texts and in a position of subservience (at least in appearance) thus emerged in the Eastern Han (25–220). Since then, few canonical classical texts were read without their commentaries, and this commentarial corpus grew as later commentators added their own commentaries to the existing corpus. Inversely, commentaries also canonised the texts that were commentated upon, for commentaries themselves affirmed that these texts were worthy of extensive critical engagement. Over time, the texts that were commentated on (i.e., the canon of classical Chinese literature in a broad sense) also expanded, later including, for instance, Buddhist texts, medieval poetry and Ming Qing fiction.[30]

Chinese terms for commentary tell us much about its forms and hermeneutic nature: 注 *zhu*, 'annotations' (often used in the expression 注釋 *zhushi*, 'annotations and explanations'), also glossed as 傳 *zhuan*, 'transmit', which is notably a synonym for 譯 *yi* 'translation'; 訓詁 *xungu*, 'glossing, using contemporary language that is easily understood to explain ancient expressions'; and 疏 *shu*, 'sub-commentary', a later developed form of commentary that reinterpreted the classical text and its primary (i.e. earlier) commentaries.[31] These various commentaries give glosses, identify allusions and citations, paraphrase in plainer language and interpret difficult parts of the primary classical text, as well as provide critical assessment of previous commentaries. The presentation of commentaries is interlinear, i.e., immediately following the primary text and inserted between sentences and breaks. In post-Tang (from 907) printed editions of classical texts, commentaries were also printed in smaller characters than the primary text to show deference to and differentiate from it. To return to the *Zhuangzi* as an example, Figures 1.1 and 1.2 show two pages with text and commentary from a reproduced *Zhuangzi* edition with commentary (*zhu*) by Guo Xiang and sub-commentary (*shu*) by 成玄英 Cheng Xuanying (c. 608–699).

As the figures show, the way commentary is written and presented is fragmented. It disrupts the flow of text and obliges the reader to oscillate between the main text and a variety of explanations that often present different commentators' views, including the later commentator's responses to earlier commentators (e.g., in Figures 1.1 and 1.2, Cheng responds to Guo Xiang and points out Guo's interpretation in fact contradicts the *Zhuangzi*'s views). Reading commentaries is therefore layered, studious and effort-requiring, an extreme form of close reading as well as slow reading.

Although this 'critical genre' of interlinear commentary grew out of Han literati's need to elucidate ancient texts, which had become 'difficult and problematic' for them after 'changes over the centuries . . . in language' (Gardner 1998: 401), the purpose and function of commentary were never merely to explain what ancient texts originally meant. Despite the apparent fragmented and inserted format of commentary, commentary presents

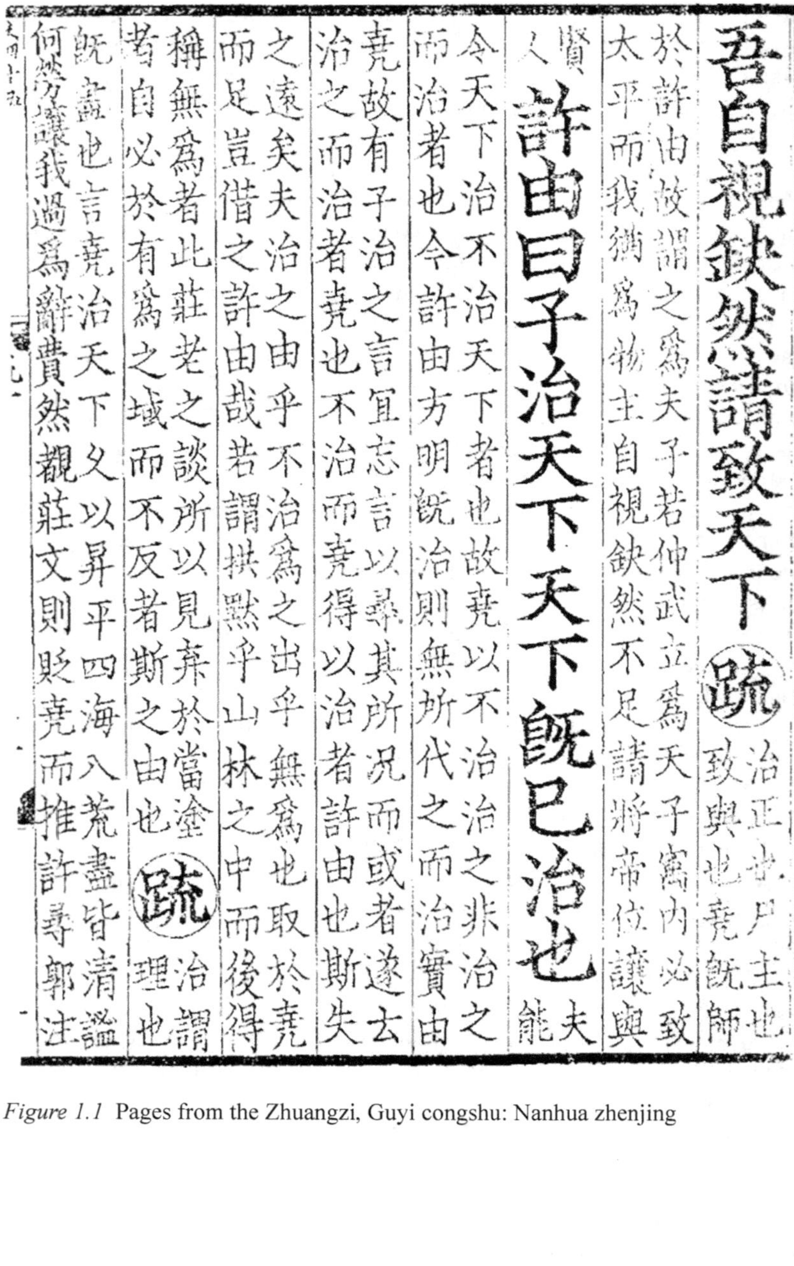

吾自視缺然請致天下疏治正也尸主也致與也堯既師於許由故謂之爲夫子若仲武立爲天子寓内必致太平而我猶爲物主自視缺然不足請將帝位讓與賢人

許由曰子治天下天下既已治也

夫能令天下治不治天下者也故堯以不治治之非治之而治者也今許由方明既治則無所代之而治實由堯故有子治之言宜忘言以尋其所況而或者遂云治之而治者堯也不治而堯得以治者許由也斯失之遠矣夫治之由乎不治爲之出乎無爲也取於堯而足豈借之許由哉若謂拱默乎山林之中而後得稱無爲者此莊老之談所以見棄於當塗當塗者自必於有爲之域而不反者斯之由也疏治謂理也既治也言堯治天下久以昇平四海八荒盡皆清謐何勞讓我過爲辭費然覩莊文則貶堯而推許尋郭注

Figure 1.1 Pages from the Zhuangzi, Guyi congshu: Nanhua zhenjing

逍遙遊一

乃弟許而優堯者何耶欲明放勳大聖仲武大賢賢
弊一塗相去遠矣故堯負衰汾陽而喪天下許由不
夷其俗而獨立高山圓照偏溺斷可知矣是以莊子
機禪讓之迹故有爝火之談郭生察無待之心要致
合義宜尋其旨況無所稍嫌也
不洽之說可謂採微索隱了文
而我猶代子吾
將為名乎名者實之賓也吾將為賓乎

夫自任者對物而順物者與物無對矣故堯無對於天
下而許由與接輿為匹矣何以言其然邪夫＿物冥
者故群物之所不能離也是以無心玄應唯感之從
況乎若不繫
者若不繫而東西之非己也故無行而不與百
姓共者亦無往而不爲天下之君矣以此爲君若天
之自高實君之德也若獨亢然立乎高山之頂非夫
人有情於自守守一家之偏尚何得專此此故俗中
之一物而爲堯之外臣耳若以外代乎内主斷南

arguments about the primary text, striving to establish a 'consistent' meaning (Wagner 2016: 498) for the primary text through the commentator's systematic interpretation. This explains why, since the Han, commentators have, through writing commentary, engaged in scholastic wrangling with their contemporaries and predecessors (Makeham 2003; Wagner 2000), for what is at stake is not word-by-word glosses or annotations for archaic terms but rivalling interpretations of the canon. Moreover, commentary explained ancient texts in a contemporary language understood by the commentator and his audience, catering to their contemporary intellectual context and needs, sometimes at the cost of misreading the primary text.[32] Guo Xiang's commentary of the *Zhuangzi*, for instance, is known for its highly distorting interpretation that goes against the grain of the *Zhuangzi* at some points to fit Guo's neo-Daoist agenda.[33] Finally, commentary not only asserts the authority and value of the commented text, thus fundamentally shaping its reception and formation as a canon, it also gives value to the commentator and his scholarly community. Commentaries accumulated over time become inseparable from the primary text and constitute an exegetical tradition on which later commentators would like to leave their own imprint. It must be noted that in premodern China, literary activities – especially the engagement with canonical ancient texts – were dominated by the literati class. The commentator enjoyed high visibility (literally, in the way commentaries are presented) and much recognition for his exegetical work. Writing commentary thus not only asserted one's credentials and status as literatus (Gardner 1998: 404) but also addressed one's own peers and scholarly group. In other words, commentary was written by and for the literati, who were well versed in extant literature and skilled in writing classical Chinese.

How does commentary then relate to translation? The two are similar and share certain features: both have an explanatory and interpretive function, both reword the primary text (or 'original text') in a language that differs from that of the primary text and both serve as a mediation across time and transfer meaning into a new semantic and historical context. Not only does commentary provide calques and paraphrases that linguistically provide matching terms for ancient expressions, like translation, commentary can produce a systematic and particular interpretation of the primary text that influences its readers' perception and plays an important role in the primary text's reception. Important commentaries in Chinese literary history – Wang Bi's commentary on the *Laozi*, Cheng Xuanying's on the *Zhuangzi*, Zhu Xi's on the *Analects* – are known for their style, interpretive approach and underlying intellectual orientations, the same aspects for which remarkable translations are remembered. Moreover, commentary sometimes directly involved translational activities: annotative (注*zhu*) commentary in the early medieval period – also the time of massive translation of Buddhist literature

– 'approximate[d] dictionaries or encyclopedias as they strive[d] to encompass different ways of understanding the text' (Cheng 2017: 130–131), and dictionaries are by nature a (self-)translational reference; sub-commentary (疏 *shu*), in addition, possibly emerged through records about debates about Buddhist sutras as they were translated, as Makeham (2003: 88) observes after Jorgensen. If we think of Chinese terms denoting 'translation', they also partially overlap with terms for commentary, such as 傳 *zhuan* mentioned earlier, and 翻譯 *fanyi* – the standard modern term of 'translation' and 'interpretation' that started appearing in medieval Buddhist texts, the 隋書 *Suishu*, and 舊唐書 *Jiu Tangshu* (Alleton 2004: 17) – instead of denoting creating in another language a full equivalent to the original text, emphasises 're-arranging', 'changing back and forth' and 'selecting' (as mentioned in the general introduction) existing textual materials, which are precisely what commentarial practices involve. If we accept that 'one representation is a translation of another if (and only if) it both refers to and paraphrases the other' (Hanks 2014: 23), then we may affirm that commentary is a readerly and writerly practice of a translational nature.

We may now understand why some Chinese scholars like Ji believe that reading commentary allows readers to understand ancient texts without taking recourse to modern Chinese translations. This view still remains problematic because, as described earlier, commentary does not provide straightforward explanations of the primary text, and the ability to read commentaries skilfully, discern their arguments and assess their nuances also needs much cultivation. In fact, reading ancient texts with only their commentaries gives the false impression of having more 'direct' access to ancient texts when this access still relies on the translational mediation of commentaries. Considering the translational nature of commentary, therefore, commentary is not less intralingually translational than modern Chinese translations. Zethsen (2009: 809) points out that intralingual translation 'is generally motivated by one or more of the key parameters; knowledge, time, culture, and space'. All these parameters underlie the creation of both commentary and modern Chinese translations, to the effect that they not only bridge the linguistic and historical gap but also 'draw a border' (Brems 2018: 510) between the ancient and contemporary, making visible the alterity of antiquity, which is why such intralingual translation is necessary in the first place. In this sense, like commentary, translation creates a relation between the ancient text and modern readers, and modern Chinese translations are, to an extent, also commentarial just as commentary is translational.

But what, then, is the difference between translation and commentary? For they must differ in some aspects to explain the decline of commentary and the rise of modern Chinese translations in the twentieth century.

To clarify this question, referring to aspects of commentary other than explaining and rewording gives us good clues to its distinction from modern translations. Firstly, in terms of format and presentation, commentary and translation diverge widely and frame the reading experience differently. Translation – especially in its published format – is a continuous and complete text, whereas commentary is interrupting and fragmentary. Translation aims to deliver a flow of consistent meaning even in the absence of the original text, whereas commentary not only makes the primary text visibly larger but also deliberately disrupts the reading process to oblige the reader to dwell on particular words and interpretive ambiguities. Commentary is also inter-commentarial – often including other commentaries one responds to and compiling different annotations into one collection (e.g., 集解 *jijie* / 集釋 *jishi* 'Collected commentaries' editions of ancient texts) – therefore constituting a dialogical and comparative way of reading. In contrast, although translators often refer to other translations and interpretations when producing their own translation, the final product does not simultaneously print those referenced translations for the reader to see. This format of translation models after the format of the 'book' as shaped by the modern publishing industry, to which modern readers are also accustomed. But the format and modern notion of 'book' – a written work giving a coherent narrative or argument and with a beginning and end – differ significantly from the material form and generic categories of much classical Chinese literature like the *Zhuangzi*.[34] Modern Chinese translations therefore dress up ancient texts in the book format, making the ancient more contemporary and relatable to modern readers and rendering their foreignness more invisible. This also means that translation reflects the adaptation to a new literary format and mode of literary production that are different from those that suited commentary. Secondly, the target readers of commentary and translation are very different. Translation is meant to be, at least can be, a replacement for the original text. Modern Chinese translations, in particular, target readers who cannot read the original text, aiming to widen access to the ancient literature that was jealously guarded by scholar-officials in the past. But commentary cannot be read without the primary text and was never meant to replace the latter since commentary was written for literati readers who could engage with the most sophisticated exegeses of the primary text. In brief, commentary is exclusive and for the scholarly elite, whereas translation is potentially for general, even uninformed readers who lack linguistic and historical background knowledge. Lastly, the motives and intellectual contexts of commentators and translators also differ. Premodern commentators, particularly from the Han to the Six Dynasties, did not have a 'default position' of being 'faithful' or subservient to the original ancient text (Puett 2009: 72). Some of them even altered the original text for more desirable interpretations. Fidelity and the acceptance of the original text in a fixed form are, however, the default position of the modern translator. Moreover, the latter's motive is no longer to establish herself within an elite social class, nor to argue with a limited circle of highly knowledgeable peers. The scholastic culture and style of scholarship that supported commentary have become obsolete. The two motives for writing commentary – to explain the primary text in more accessible language and to respond to and argue with one's peers' interpretations – may be understood as having transformed into translation on the one hand and sinology on the other.

We can now answer the question why premodern Chinese readers of the *Zhuangzi* and other classical Chinese texts did not produce translations: because commentary served a translational function and met the needs of a select group of literati readers. As for why modern Chinese translations emerged in the twentieth century while commentary declined, there are certainly many historical reasons to cite. In particular, language reforms, from the anti-classical Chinese discourse of the New Culture Movement to the standardisation of modern written Chinese based on spoken Mandarin in the 1950s,[35] have exponentially raised literacy rates to expand the potential readership of classical Chinese literature to the general public. Nevertheless, classical Chinese is no longer a state-sponsored written language, and the extensive study of classical literature has become a specialised academic field rather than an obligatory part of one's general education (as was the case for premodern educated classes). In this context, translating classical Chinese literature like the *Zhuangzi* into modern standard Chinese fundamentally democratises literature and changes the reading experience, which constitutes a distanciation from premodern commentarial scholarship. Modern Chinese translations are themselves an aspect of Chinese literary modernity that translates the tradition of premodern China and makes ancient texts contemporary.

Conclusion

Modern translations of classical Chinese literature reveal a field of translational visibilities and invisibilities involving the reception of Chinese classics in East Asia and beyond, processes of intralingual and cross-period translation and hermeneutic and historical connections between commentary, translation, and Chinese modernity. The *Zhuangzi*, as the example here, shows itself to be particularly open to different translational strategies and constraints that bring esoteric language and inexhaustible translatability into play. Multiple and proliferating translations of the *Zhuangzi* render the text both more visible and invisible: visible in the sense of creating more facets of meaning, constantly generating interest and more widely read, and invisible in the sense that the 'original' text of the *Zhuangzi* is increasingly pluralised and becomes more and more inscrutable through its accumulated layers of translations. All these translations and readings do not produce a 'synthesis' but an 'unruly hold-all of the manifold' (Scott 2012: 62), like Cézanne's Mont Sainte-Victoire paintings. But this plurality and inscrutability created by a series of translational and interpretive procedures have always already happened for the *Zhuangzi* (as well as for other canonical classical Chinese texts like the *Daodejing* and 楚辭 *Chuci*), through the commentarial tradition. Besides relating to modern Chinese translations of classical literature through its intralingually translational dimension, premodern commentary helps us rethink the notion of translation in the Chinese context as different degrees of rewordings and selective reconfigurations of existing expressions and texts rather than creating a whole new text that resembles faithfully the original text. Seen in this light, the difference between intralingual and interlingual translation is indeed more 'a question of degree than of kind' (Zethsen 2009: 795). This is why reading multiple translations comparatively is important – a reading method that takes inspiration from the dialogical and inter-commentarial way in which commentaries were read – for comparison allows aspects rendered more or less visible by translation to show against each other. We may then understand (in)visibility in and of translation as multiple and uneven, a question of differentiation, emphasis, and noticeability rather than an opposition between the self and other, presence and absence.

Notes

1 Here, the term 'literature' is used in the broad sense of 'writing' since Western literary genres that separate philosophical, religious and 'belles lettres' literature, such as poetry and fiction, do not apply well to premodern Chinese texts.
2 The other three canonical Daoist texts given the name of 經 *jing*, 'classic' are the *Daodejing*, the 列子 *Liezi* and the 文子 *Wenzi*.
3 Some recent scholarship has noted the under-studiedness of intralingual translation, e.g. workshop and book project on 'Intralingual translation, diglossia and the rise of vernaculars in East Asian classical and premodern cultures': https://intraling-asia.sciencesconf.org/resource/page/id/4 [accessed 18 July 2018].
4 Pre-1950s English translators' preference for classics is noted by Laughlin 2013. This preference also applies to French and German translations of Chinese texts, see Chan (2003).
5 Refer to Chapters 2 and 3 for discussion about classical Chinese learning in Japan and Korea.
6 For discussions about the *Zhuangzi*'s authorship and possible datation, see Liu (1994) and Klein (2010).
7 Sima Qian, 史記 *Shiji* chapter 63.
8 The fifty-two chapter edition of the *Zhuangzi* was defined by the Han imperial librarian 劉向 Liu Xiang (79–8/77–6 BCE), and the division of Inner, Outer and Miscellaneous Chapters already existed in the Han (although not in the form of Guo's edition).

9 See Liu (2015) on Zhuangzi's presence in modern writers such as Zhou Zuoren, Han Shaogong and Yan Lianke.
10 See Chen (2011) on the National Studies craze.
11 Some notable modern Japanese translations accompanied with commentaries are 福永光司 《庄子译注》 (1956), 津四左右吉 《庄子内篇译解》 (1966), 《庄子外篇译解》 (1966), 阿部吉雄 《庄子译注》 (1968), 森三树三郎 《老子·庄子》 (译注)(1968), 金谷治 《庄子内篇译注》 (1971), 和 《庄子译注》 (1973), 赤塚忠 《庄子译注》 (1974).
12 See McCormack (2007).
13 See Ng's unpublished thesis (2012) for a comprehensive list of English translations of the *Zhuangzi*.
14 Several recent studies that take distinctly new approaches to the *Zhuangzi* include Mcgraw (2010), Li (2015a), and Moeller and D'Ambrosio (2017).
15 The *Analects*, for instance, has over forty English translations, while the *Daodejing*'s Western translations are estimated at over 250.
16 References to *Zhuangzi* chapters and sections follow the digital library Ctext.org (e.g. 12.3 means chapter 12 section 3), and Wang Shumin's edition of the *Zhuangzi* (莊子校詮, 2007)is used for original text citations.
17 See Sato (2017) for the explanation of *kakikudashibun*.
18 See Fuehrer and Wong (2015) for more about translation and the emergence of sinology.
19 Only premodern Chinese texts are printed in traditional script by a few mainland Chinese publishers, such as Zhonghua Shuju, Shanghai Guji and Shangwu Yinshuguan. Vertical printing is only used for classical Chinese texts in mainland China. In Taiwan and Hong Kong, vertical printing is more widely used but still echoes a deliberately more archaic style. Vertical printing is, however, still very common in Japan.
20 See Girardot (1988), Lewis (2006).
21 *Diaogui* appears, however, almost exclusively in literary criticism now.
22 The most footnoted translation is Graham's, which is still very selective and does not explain the faux amis I mention. Lengthy footnotes are generally not appreciated in translations (e.g., Levi explicitly denounces it (p. 10) and uses no footnotes), and Graham's translation has been criticised for its clunkiness.
23 See the whole story in 12.4. One might raise the issue that what the sentence in 2.7 means does not need to be – even should not be – interpreted by reference to other *Zhuangzi* sections, since there is no necessary relation between different sections. Nevertheless, since I am proposing one possible interpretation that makes plausible the interpretation of 圖 as 'seek', considering other parts of the *Zhuangzi* is a legitimate alternative. Billeter (2014) has studied the 象罔 story (12.4) and argued that it coheres with many key concerns in the Inner chapters.
24 See Chen p. 190, Graham (1982: 23–24) for discussion about the insertion of this passage.
25 惠施 Hui Shi, Zhuangzi's intellectual rival that often appears in the text as a character.
26 鵷鶵 *yuanchu*, a type of male phoenix; 鴟 *chi*, a kind of carnivorous hawkish bird similar to the kite or owl, often cited for its cruelty and arrogance; 梧桐 *wutong* denotes the Chinese parasol tree, typically characterised as the phoenix's preferred perch and highly valued for its wood.

27 After the pioneering works in Old Chinese phonology by Karlgren (1957), Baxter (1992) and Sagart (1999), more recent studies include Zheng (2003), Schuessler (2009) and Baxter and Sagart (2014). Handel (in Wang and Sun 2015) gives a good summary of the findings in the field.
28 Ji in an interview about preserving Chinese traditions and simplified characters, see http://edu.people.com.cn/GB/79457/8816825.html [accessed July 2018].
29 See Denecke (2011) on Master-texts.
30 See Rolston (1997) for fiction commentary.
31 These are the most commonly used terms for commentary but not the only ones (others include 解 *jie*, 詮 *quan*, 箋 *jian*, etc.).
32 The 'misreading' character of commentaries has prompted Arthur Waley's (1934: 129) famous depreciation of them, seconded by other sinologists, such as Billeter (2004), who is quite dismissive of premodern *Zhuangzi* commentaries.
33 See Ziporyn (2003) on Guo Xiang.
34 For the early Chinese category of 書 *shu*, which differs from its modern Chinese meaning as 'book', see Allan (2012).
35 See Shang (2014) for the artificial opposition between *baihua* and *wenyanwen*.

Bibliography

Zhuangzi *editions and translations*

Arena, Leonardo Vittorio. 2009. *Zhuangzi*. Milan: Biblioteca Univ. Rizzoli.
Buber, Martin. 1910. *Reden und gleichnisse des Tschuang-tse*. Leipzig: Insel-Verlag.
Chen Guying. 2009. 莊子今注今譯 (3 vols.). Beijing: Zhonghua shuju.
Fang Yong. 2015. 庄子. Beijing: Zhonghua shuju, 2nd reprint.
Graham, Angus C. 1981/2001. *Chuangtzu: The Inner Chapters*. Indianapolis: Hackett, reprint.
Hara Tomio. 1962. *Sōshi: Gendai goyaku*. Tokyo: Shunjūsha.
Kōzen Hiroshi and Fukunaga Mitsuji. 2013. 莊子. Tokyo: Chikuma Shobō.
Laurenti, Carlo and Christine Leverd (translated from Liou 1969). 1992. *Zhuang-zi*. Milan: Adelphi.
Levi, Jean. 2006/2010. *Les Œuvres de Maître Tchouang* (revised ed.). Paris: Editions de l'Encyclopédie des Nuisances.
Liou Kia-hway. 1969. *Tchouang-tseu: Œuvre complète*. Paris: Gallimard.
Mair, Victor. 1998. *Wandering on the Way: Early Taoist Tales and Parables of Chuang Tzu*. Honolulu: University of Hawai'i Press.
Nutrizio, P. 2011. *L'Opera di Chuang Tzu*. Milan: Luni Editrice.
Sabbadini, Augusto. 2012. *Chuang Tzu*. Milan: Feltrinelli.
Stange, Hans. 1954. *Tschuang-tse, Dichtung und Weisheit*. Wiesbaden: Insel.
Vávra, Dušan. 2017. 'Translating Early Chinese Texts and the Problem of Contextualization: The Example of Chapter 1 of the Lǎozǐ'. *Acta Universitatis Carolinae: Philologica* 4: 63–84.
Venuti, Lawrence. 1995. *The Translator's Invisibility: A History of Translation*. London and New York: Routledge.
Wang Shumin. 2007. 莊子校詮. Beijing: Zhonghua shuju.
Watson, Burton. 1968. *The Complete Works of Chuang Tzu*. New York: Columbia University Press.

Wilhelm, Richard. 1912. *Dschuang Dsi: Das wahre Buch vom südlichen Blütenland*. Jena: Diederichs.
The Zhuangzi. Ctext digital database: https://ctext.org/zhuangzi [accessed March–July 2018].
Ziporyn, Brook. 2009. *Zhuangzi: The Essential Writings*. Indianapolis: Hackett.

Secondary references

Akatsuka, Kiyoshi. 1974. *Soshi, in Zenshaku kanbun taikei* [Fully interpreted Chinese literature series], vols 16–17, Tokyo: Shuesha.
Allan, Sarah. 2012. 'On *Shu* 書 (Documents) and the Origin of the *Shang shu* 尚書 (Ancient Documents) in Light of Recently Discovered Bamboo Slip Manuscripts'. *Bulletin of SOAS* 75 (3): 547–557.
Alleton, Viviane. 2004. 'Traduction et conceptions chinoises de texte écrit'. *Etudes chinoises* 23: 9–43.
Apter, Emily. 2013. *Against World Literature*. New York: Verso.
Baxter, William. 1992. *A Handbook of Old Chinese Phonology*. Berlin: Mouton de Gruyter.
Baxter, William and Laurent Sagart. 2014. *Old Chinese: A New Reconstruction*. Oxford: Oxford University Press.
Brems, Elke. 2018. 'Separated by the Same Language: Intralingual Translation between Dutch and Dutch', *Perspectives* 26 (4): 509–525.
Billeter, Jean-François. 2004. *Etudes sur Tchouang-tseu*. Paris: Allia.
Billeter, Jean-François. 2014. *Leçons sur Tchouang-tseu*, Paris: Allia.
Chan, Tak-Hung Leo, ed. *One into Many: Translation and the Dissemination of Classical Chinese Literature*. Amsterdam: Rodopi, 2003.
Chen Jianming. 2011. 'The National Studies Craze'. *China Perspectives* (1): 22–30.
Cheng Yu-yu. 2017. 'Text and Commentary in the Medieval Period'. In *The Oxford Handbook of Classical Chinese Literature*, ed. Wiebke Denecke, Wai-yee Li, and Xiaofei Tian. New York: Oxford University Press, 123–131.
Childs, Margaret and Nancy Hope, eds. 2015. *Voices of East Asia: Essential Readings from Antiquity to the Present*. New York: Routledge.
Chou Chih-Ping. 2007. 'Teaching Classical Chinese through Modern Chinese'. *Journal of the Chinese Language Teachers Association* 42 (2): 85–94.
Denecke, Wiebke. 2011. *The Dynamics of Masters Literature*. Cambridge, MA: Harvard University Asia Center.
Feng, Youlan. 1931. *Chuang Tzŭ: A New Selected Translation with an Exposition of the Philosophy of Kuo Hsiang*. Shanghai: The Commercial Press Ltd.
Fuehrer, Bernhard and Lawrence Wang-chi Wong, eds. 2015. *Sinologists as Translators in the Seventeenth to Nineteenth Centuries*. Hong Kong: The Chinese University Press.
Fukunaga, Mitsuji. 1956. *Sōshi* 6 Volumes. Tokyo: Asahi.
Gardner, Daniel K. 1998. 'Confucian Commentary and Chinese Intellectual History'. *The Journal of Asian Studies* 57 (2): 397–422.
Giles, Herbert. 1889. *Chuang Tzu: Mystic, Moralist, and Social Reformer*, London: Bernard Quaritch.

Girardot, Norman. 1988. *Myth and Meaning in Early Taoism*. Berkeley, Los Angeles and London: University of California Press.

Graham, Angus. 1982. *Chuang-tzu: Textual Notes to a Partial Translation*. London: SOAS.

Handel, Zev. 2015. 'Old Chinese Phonology'. In *The Oxford Handbook of Chinese Linguistics*, ed. William Wang and Chaofen Sun. New York: Oxford University Press, 68–79.

Hanks, William. 2014. 'The Space of Translation'. *Hau: Journal of Ethnographic Theory* 4 (2): 17–39.

Harbsmeier, Christoph. 2012. 'Plurality and the Sub-Classification of Nouns in Classical Chinese'. In *Plurality and Classifiers across Languages in China*, ed. Dan Xu. Berlin and Boston: De Gruyter, 121–142.

Jakobson, Roman. (1959) 2004. 'On Linguistic Aspects of Translation'. In *The Translation Studies Reader* (2nd ed.), ed. Lawrence Venuti. London: Routledge, 138–143.

Jung Jae-seo. 2000. 'Daoism in Korea'. In *Daoism Handbook*, ed. Livia Kohn. Leiden, Boston and Koln: Brill.

Kame Setsuko and Patrick Sautreuil. 2013. 'Signification de la "Leçon sur Tchouang-tseu" au Japon'. *Acupuncture & Moxibustion* 12 (1): 73–75.

Karlgren, Bernhard. 1957. *Grammatica serica resensa*. Stockholm: Museum of Far Eastern Antiquities.

Kim, Tong-song. 1963. *Changja*, Sŏul Tˊŭkpyŏlsi: Ŭryu Munhwasa.

Kim, Tal-chin. 1968. *Changja*, Sŏul: Hyŏnamsa.

Klein, Esther. 2010. 'Were There "Inner Chapters" in the Warring States? A New Examination of Evidence about the *Zhuangzi*'. *T'oung Pao*, Second Series, 96 (4/5): 299–369.

Komjathy, Louis. 2004. 'Daoist Texts in Translation'. *Advanced Resources for Daoist Studies*. https://archive.li/bD86P [accessed July 2018], 1–70.

Laughlin, Charles. 2013. 'The New Translators and Contemporary Chinese Literature in English'. *Clear* 35: 209–214.

Legge, James. 1891. *The Sacred Books of China: the Texts of Taoism*, Oxford: Clarendon Press.

Lewis, Mark Edward. 2006. *The Flood Myths of Early China*. Albany: SUNY Press.

Li, Xiaofan Amy. 2015a. *Comparative Encounters between Artaud, Michaux and the* Zhuangzi. Oxford: Legenda.

Li, Xiaofan Amy. 2015b. 'The Notion of Originality and Degrees of Faithfulness in Translating Classical Chinese: Comparing Translations of the *Liezi*'. *Early China* 38: 109–128.

Li, Xiaofan Amy. 2017. 'When Do Different Literatures Become Comparable?'. In *Minding Borders*, ed. Adriana X. Jacobs, Matthew Reynolds, et al. Cambridge: Legenda.

Liu Jianmei. 2015. *Zhuangzi and Modern Chinese Literature*. Oxford: Oxford University Press.

Liu Lydia H. 1995. *Translingual Practice: Literature, National Culture, and Translated Modernity: China, 1900–1937*. Stanford: Stanford University Press.

Liu Weijie. 2011. '说古文今译'. *Journal of Weifang University* 11 (5): 67–69.

Liu Xiaogan. 1994. *Classifying the* Zhuangzi *Chapters*, trans. William Savage. Ann Arbor: University of Michigan Press.
Lowenthal, David. 1985. *The Past is a Foreign Country*. Cambridge: Cambridge University Press.
Mair, Victor H. 1994. 'Introduction and Notes for a Complete Translation of the *Chuang Tzu*'. *Sino-Platonic Papers* 48: 1–110.
Makeham, John. 2003. *Transmitters and Creators: Chinese Commentators and Commentaries on the Analects*. Cambridge, MA: Harvard University Asia Center.
McCormack, Jerusha. 2007. 'From Chinese Wisdom to Irish Wit: Zhuangzi and Oscar Wilde'. *Irish University Review* 37 (2): 302–321.
Mcgraw, David. 2010. *Stratifying Zhuangzi: Rhyme and Other Quantitative Evidence*. Taipei: Institute of Linguistics, Academia Sinica.
Michaux, Henri. 1936. Entre Centre et Absence. H. Matarasso.
Moeller, Hans-Georg and Paul D'Ambrosio. 2017. *Genuine Pretending: On the Philosophy of the Zhuangzi*. New York: Columbia University Press.
Møllgaard, Eske. 2007. *An Introduction to Daoist Thought*. Abingdon and New York: Routledge.
Ng Ka Yi. 2012. 'A Research of the English-Speaking World's Philological Studies of *Zhuangzi*'. unpublished PhD Thesis, The Chinese University of Hong Kong.
Osamu, Kanaya. 1971. *Sōshi* 4 Volumes. Iwanami Bunko.
Palmer, Martin, Elizabeth Breuilly, Wai Ming Chang, Jay Ramsay. 1996. *The Book of Chuang Tzu*, London: Arkana.
Peyraube, Alain. 2016. 'Ancient Chinese'. In *The Routledge Encyclopedia of the Chinese Language*, ed. Sin-wai Chan. Oxford and New York: Routledge, 1–17.
Pratt, Keith and Richard Rutt. 2013. *Korea: A Historical and Cultural Dictionary*. Surrey: Curzon, Press.
Puett, Michael. 2009. 'Sages, Gods, and History: Commentarial Strategies in Late Chinese Antiquity'. *Antiquorum Philosophia* 3: 71–88.
Puett, Michael. 2017. 'Text and Commentary: The Early Tradition'. In *The Oxford Handbook of Classical Chinese Literature*, ed. Wiebke Denecke, Wai-yee Li, and Xiaofei Tian. New York: Oxford University Press, 112–122.
Pulleyblank, Edwin. 1995. *Outline of Classical Chinese Grammar*. Vancouver: UBC Press.
Qiu Peipei. 2005. *Bashō and the Dao: The* Zhuangzi *and the Transformation of Haikai*. Honolulu: University of Hawai'i Press.
Rolston, David. 1997. *Traditional Chinese Fiction and Fiction Commentaries*. Stanford: Stanford University Press.
Sagart, Laurent. 1999. *The Roots of Old Chinese*. Amsterdam: Benjamins.
Sato Katsuyuki. 2017. 'Kundoku-bun: A Hybrid Genre in Japanese Literature'. In *Mapping Genres, Mapping Culture*, ed. Elizabeth Thomson et al. John Benjamins Publishing.
Saussy, Haun. 2017. *Translation as Citation: The* Zhuangzi *Inside Out*. Oxford: Oxford University Press.
Schuessler, Axel. 2009. *Minimal Old Chinese and Later Han Chinese*. Honolulu: University of Hawai'i Press.
Scott, Clive. 2012. *Translating the Perception of Text*. Oxford: Legenda.

Shang Wei. 2014. 'Writing and Speech: Rethinking the Issue of Vernaculars in Early Modern China'. In *Rethinking East Asian Languages, Vernaculars, and Literacies, 1000–1919*, ed. Benjamin Elman. Leiden: Brill, 254–301.

Van Norden, Bryan. 2009. 'Review of *Zhuangzi: The Essential Writings with Selections from Traditional Commentaries* by Brook Ziporyn'. *China Review International* 16 (1): 147–150.

Wagner, Rudolf. 2000. *The Craft of a Chinese Commentator: Wang Bi on the Laozi*. Albany: SUNY Press.

Wagner, Rudolf. 2016. 'Rules for the Construction of Meaning: "Translations" by Chinese Commentators'. In *Open Horizon: Essays in Honour of Wolfgang Kubin*, ed. by Li Xuetao et al. Beijing: Foreign Language Teaching and Research Press and Duesseldorf: Duesseldorf University Press, 489–504.

Waley, Arthur. 1934. *The Way and Its Power*. London: Allen & Unwin.

Wieger, Léon. 1913. *Les Pères du système taoïste*, vol. 3, Shanghai: Imprimerie de Hien Hien.

Wu Kuang-ming. 1982. *Chuang tzu: World Philosopher at Play*. New York, NY: Crossroad Publishing Company; Chico, CA: Scholars Press.

Yan Lingfeng. 1993. *周秦汉魏诸子知见书目*. Beijing: Zhonghua shuju.

Zádrapa, Lukáś. 2011. *Word-Class Flexibility in Classical Chinese: Verbal and Adverbial Uses of Nouns*. Leiden: Brill.

Zethsen, Karen Korning. 2009. 'Intralingual Translation: An Attempt at Description'. *Meta: Journal des Traducteurs* 54: 795–812.

Zhang, Ai-min. 2005. 'On the Acceptance to Zhuangzi of Critics in the Song Dynasty'. *Journal of Teachers College Qingdao University* 1: 60–63.

Zhang, Aimin, 2005. '*莊子在日本的傳播*' /'The reception of the Zhuangzi in Japan.' *Journal of Shandong Normal University* (Humanities and Social Sciences), vol. 50 no. 2 (General No. 199), pp. 12–17.

Zhao Yuanren. 1980. *语言问题*. Beijing, Shangwu.

Zheng Zhangshangfang. 2003. *上古音系*. Shanghai: Shanghai Jiaoyu Press.

Ziporyn Brook. 2003. *The Penumbra Unbound: The Neo-Taoist Philosophy of Guo Xiang*. Albany: SUNY Press.

2 Layered translations

Glossing, adaptation and the reception of Bai Juyi's poetry in premodern Japan

Jennifer Guest

Introduction

The reception of classical Chinese texts in premodern Japan offers a chance to think about the complex array of translation-like activity – gloss-based reading, remixing, poetic adaptation, vernacular retelling – involved in the evolving relationship between two very different literary languages. This chapter considers how a concept of translation might stretch to describe this linguistic space and its literary possibilities and asks what there might be to learn here about writing, reading, literary reception and language contact.

Considering questions about premodern Japanese language and literature through the lens of contemporary English creates its own layer of translation issues, rendering certain categories more or less visible; neither 'language' nor 'literature' has a single exact and unassailable equivalent in Heian Japanese, and this is clearly true of 'translation' as well. Although in modern Japanese *hon'yaku* (翻訳) is well established as a calque for English 'translation', it was rarely used in premodern sources and tended to have a specialised association with the large official projects of Chinese sutra translation. Instead, a wide variety of other terms were used situationally to describe engagements with texts brought from the continent,[1] including terms that focus on calligraphic style, commentarial explication, casual/vernacular interpretation and other features that might not automatically be considered within the bounds of translation narrowly defined. As a starting point, I will keep in view the diverse set of practices involved in working with texts from a very different linguistic context and consider them loosely as 'translational', with the aim that a constant awareness of working back and forth between disparate sets of categories may help make some new connections and contrasts visible.

Beyond the familiar comparative tensions around using terms like 'literature' and 'translation' in a premodern Japanese setting, talking about 'Chinese texts' or Chinese-style writing (*kanbun* 漢文) as a trigger for translation presents an extra set of problems. At the core of this issue is *kundoku* (訓読), a semi-standardised system of gloss-based reading and writing that allowed classical Chinese texts to be read as a distinctive style of Japanese while continuing to visually reflect the source language – and conversely allow the creation of 'classical Chinese' written texts that adhere in some degree to shared regional standards but are firmly rooted in Japanese language. Kundoku-based reading and writing challenges simple assumptions about the potential relationships between language and writing, as well as about the potential dynamics of language contact; it involves practices of 'translation' that are built up collaboratively over time, displaced from an interlingual to an intralingual (or intersemiotic) ground or folded invisibly into the transition between writing and speech. Similar kinds of literacy played an important role in the adoption of classical Chinese-style texts throughout East Asia, and there are also parallels elsewhere in the premodern world, giving the question of translation in premodern Japan much broader linguistic and literary significance.[2]

Modern scholarship on kundoku has been haunted by the problem of defining it in relation to translation or to the Japanese term *hon'yaku*, a problem inextricably connected to understandings of East Asian literacies. The diverging analyses of two leading scholars in this area make for a good illustration. Saitō Mareshi (2014: 95–97) argues for an important distinction between interpreting between two spoken languages (*hon'yaku*) and localisation of a written language (*kundoku*) and suggests that premodern Japanese readings of Chinese texts are better understood as a form of textual interpretation internal to the Sinographic sphere (漢字圏内部における本文解釈の一形態, p. 162). Meanwhile Nakamura Shunsaku (2014) characterises kundoku as kind of 'cultural translation' (文化の翻訳), albeit one that may seem unfamiliar to modern readers, and calls for further consideration of 'the problem(s) of a kind of "translation" distinctive to kundoku' (訓読独自の〈翻訳〉の問題).[3] The contrast between their approaches suggests the intellectual risks and rewards at stake in associating kundoku with the problematic of translation.

The fact that kundoku can be used to read Chinese characters as Japanese without any reference to Chinese language makes it appear more like a kind of reading – the translational equivalences can be drawn between written characters and Japanese words rather than between Chinese and Japanese words. However, in practice, Chinese-style readings of characters (*onyomi* 音読み) have continued to play an important role in the system and its performative use, linked to Japanese words by shared associations to written characters – which means that this kind of reading process created something like a linguistic contact zone where mediated forms of loanwords and rhetorical patterns could be readily exchanged. We are left with a mode of literacy that seems to fulfil some of the functions commonly associated with translation and a set of questions about where to draw lines between translation and interpretation, between translation and reading or between translation and language contact. There is a danger that applying a narrow model of translation as meaning transfer between two discrete languages to premodern Japanese writing could overemphasise the binary opposition of Chinese and Japanese, obscuring more complex relationships between different varieties of writing and speech,[4] but there is growing interest in the idea that kundoku generates a kind of 'translationese' or mediating translation zone within the language,[5] though the internal dynamics of this space and its connections to other linguistic and literary practices still need further research. As Brian Steininger (2017) has pointed out, the 'apparent limitations of *kundoku* when viewed from a modern conception of "translation" are not coincidental flaws, but integral to its function as ritualized linguistic performance, drawing upon and reinforcing the authority of valorized texts' (p. 209) – a concept of translation that can encompass kundoku-based reading and writing would need to pay close attention to overlapping and interconnected practices of commentary, performance and literary creation.

My aim here is not to conclusively pin down whether kundoku 'counts' as translation but to consider some questions that arise from placing the various ways of dealing with Chinese literary texts in premodern Japan into a translational frame. What kinds of linguistic knowledge and creative work are involved in reading or adapting classical Chinese texts as Japanese? What kinds of practices (reading, glossing, performing, compiling) help create reflections of Chinese texts within Japanese literature? What roles are available to 'translators' in this context, and how do they seem to understand their own task?

As a concrete setting for exploring these questions, this chapter will focus on the poems of Bai Juyi (particularly his 'New Ballads' 新楽府), which were widely read and adapted in premodern Japan and also left various traces in literary language. These poems occupied a flexible position between 'high classics' and court poetry, and they offer the chance to consider the particular intertextual dynamics at work in the translation of poetic vocabulary and form across multiple new styles of language. My main focus will be on medieval examples (over a loosely defined period from around 900–1500 CE), but it will first be helpful to look more concretely at what kundoku meant in the context of a 'New Ballads' poem and to illustrate the processes of distributed and paratextual translation that could be embedded in the act of reading this kind of text.[6]

Reading by gloss: translation in the margins

When a copy of Bai Juyi's collected works was confiscated from a ship in a Kyushu harbour and sent to the early ninth-century Heian court,[7] it began centuries of fascination with his poetry, especially his vividly drawn narrative poems like the 'Song of Lasting Sorrow (長恨歌, Ch. Chang hen ge, J. Chōgonka)' and 'New Ballads (新楽府, Ch. Xin yuefu, J. Shin gafu)'. Writers working in styles patterned on classical Chinese used Bai Juyi's vocabulary and imagery in their own compositions; writers of more localised styles of classical Japanese (including the brief form of court poetry known as *waka* 和歌) adapted and alluded to his poetry more freely. The 'New Ballads', an eclectic set of verses linked by a socially critical perspective and attention to viewpoint characters from various walks of life, were also used as an introductory poetic primer. The impact of this poetry was so pervasive that multiple scholars wrote about encountering Bai Juyi in dreams and seizing the chance to discuss his work.[8]

The majority of these readers and writers would have been unable to carry on a spoken conversation in Chinese and indeed were uninterested in doing so. Thinking about this situation as a striking case of language contact and literary exchange, it seems reasonable to ask when and how Bai Juyi's poems were translated into Japanese – but the answer is far from straightforward and opens up a wide field of different possible engagements between a classical Chinese text and forms of Japanese. For example, by the early nineteenth century many readers were encountering Bai Juyi's poetry in something like the following print form (Figures 2.1 and 2.2).

Rather than Bai Juyi's collected works, these examples are from editions of the *Japanese and Chinese-style Chanting Collection* (*Wakan rōeishū*, 和漢朗詠集), an early eleventh-century anthology that arranges couplets and other excerpts of Chinese-style writing together with waka poems by topic. This collection's role in literary education made it a key source for the transmission of Chinese poetry; since more than half of its roughly 230 Chinese couplets are by Bai Juyi, it played a considerable role in shaping the reception of his work. The variety of editions surviving from the first half of the nineteenth century reflect its continued importance. The left-hand image is from *A Commentary in Our National Characters on the Japanese- and Chinese-style Chanting Collection* compiled by Kō Ranzan (和漢朗詠国字抄, 1835 reprint),[9] and the right-hand image is from *Japanese and Chinese-style Chanting Collection, with added hiragana and explanations* (和漢朗詠集 – 平かな付講釈入, 1843) edited by Yamazaki Kyūsaku.[10] As the result of a long and varied tradition of reading classical Chinese poetry, they vividly illustrate the interconnected layers of anthologising, commentary, and literacy practices that must be untangled in order to consider the question of translation in premodern Japan.

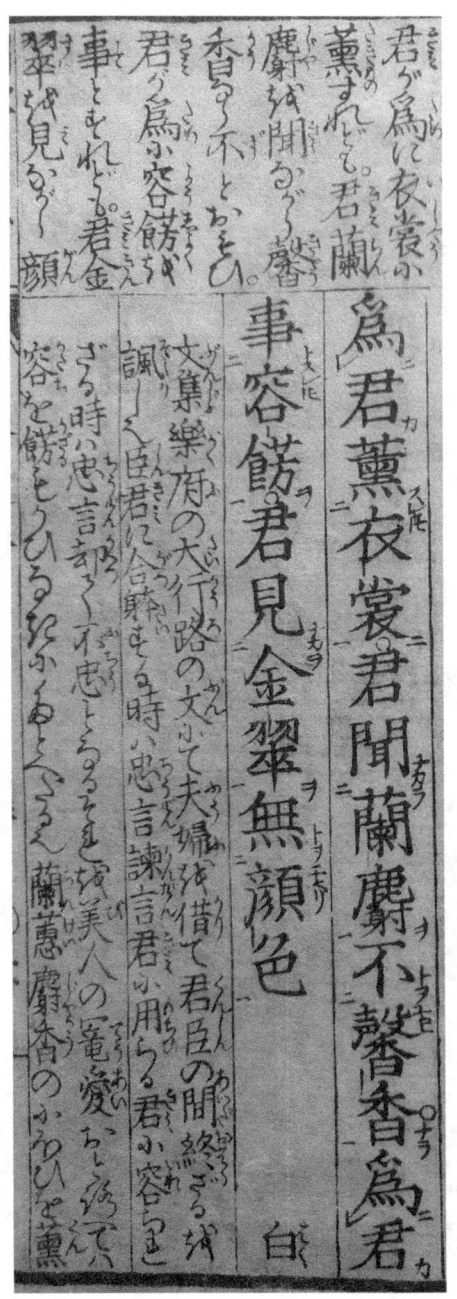

Figure 2.1 A Commentary in Our National Characters on the Japanese- and Chinese-style Chanting Collection by Kō Ranzan (和漢朗詠国字抄, 1835 reprint, preface dated 1803).

Source: Image courtesy of the author.

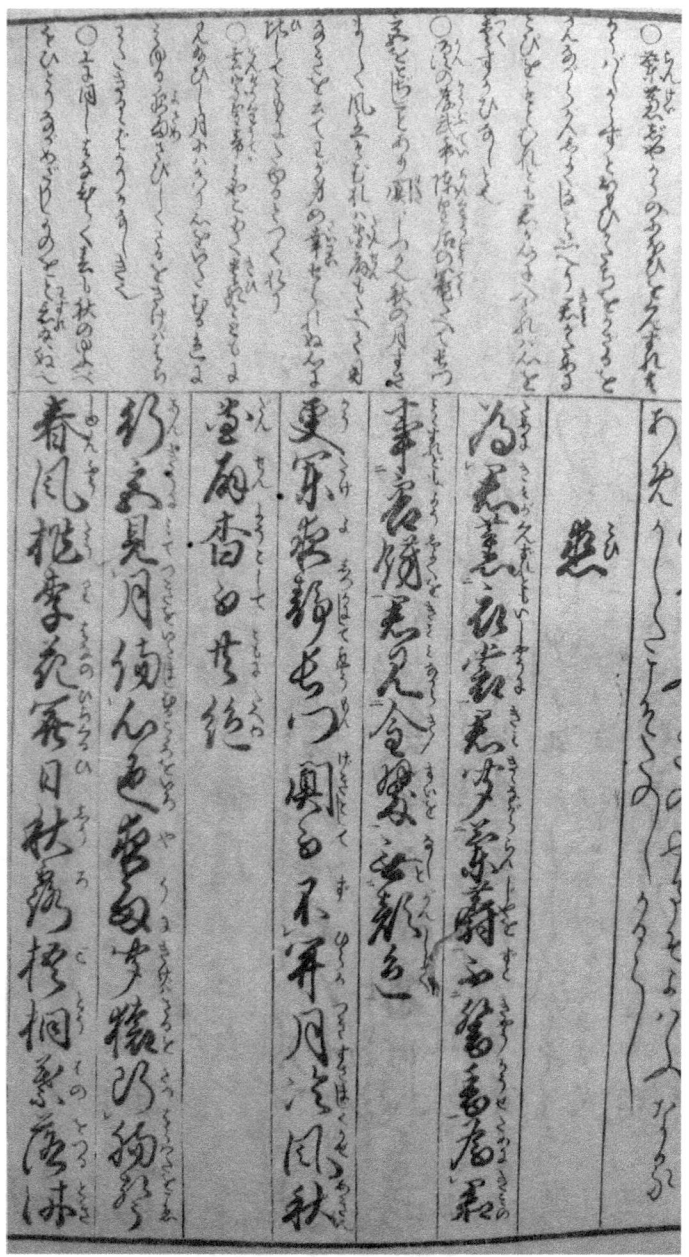

Figure 2.2 Japanese and Chinese-style Chanting Collection, with added hiragana and lecture notes by Yamazaki Kyūsaku (和漢朗詠集 – 平かな付講釈入, 1843).

Source: Images courtesy of the author.

Layered translations 55

Both editions are centred on larger characters giving a few lines from a Chinese-style poem, in this case Bai Juyi's 'The Taixing Road 太行路', a 'New Ballads' poem in the voice of a neglected wife that uses marital discord as a metaphor for a breakdown in the relationship between lord and faithful minister. These lines are then surrounded by layers of glosses and commentary. The small characters along the right edges of the characters spell out glosses in *kana* (仮名, abbreviated phonographs), and symbols along their left edges suggest changes in word order needed to create a Japanese reading. In the top margin box, conventionally a space reserved for commentary or other paratextual material, Ranzan's edition provides the reading that would be generated by his rather minimally glossed text in a more accessible style of mixed-script written Japanese, sometimes known as *kundokutai* or 'kundoku language';[11] Yamazaki's edition gives more detailed glosses on the main text in cursive *hiragana* (平仮名), sufficient to fully specify a Japanese reading, and instead uses the top margin for commentary explaining key phrases in clearer and more generally accessible language. Ranzan also adds a denser layer of commentary, following the lines of poetry in half-width characters, which includes some similar explanatory paraphrases to Yamazaki's in addition to more extensive and scholarly background information. Of the two, the layout of Ranzan's edition 'in our national characters' owes a great deal to Chinese studies traditions of making the classics accessible, according the *Chanting Collection* the dignity of a scholarly object while providing generous aid for readers;[12] Yamazaki's edition, with its emphasis on cursive script and the more streamlined type of commentarial apparatus, suggests an audience with less interest in Chinese-style scholarship and more in the collection's role as a calligraphic primer.

In both cases, a central position is reserved for the 'original text', even as the process of reading and understanding it in Japanese is distributed outward into successive layers of gloss and commentary. A summary of the various possible 'translations' on offer here, standardised in historical spellings but modern forms of *hiragana* and with key linguistic differences underlined, might look like the following table. (I also include rough translations into English, though the grammatical differences between versions need further explanation.)

The two editions clearly draw on some of the same commentarial sources, as they include exactly the same explanatory paraphrase for the second line. They also give similar renderings in Japanese at the gloss level, reflecting a shared culture of semi-standardised character associations and shared assumptions about kundoku style. The differences are also telling, however. Even within this kind of developed reading system, there are still decisions to be made between multiple possible Japanese glosses that might be

Table 2.1 Multiple translations in two editions of a Bai Juyi poem

	Ranzan's edition	Yamazaki's edition	English translation
Poem excerpt	為君薫衣裳。	君聞蘭麝不馨香。	For your sake I perfume my clothes. You breathe in orchid and musk, and don't find them fragrant.
Gloss-based reading	きみがためにいしやうに**た**きもの**す**れども、きみらんじゃをきき**ながら**けいこう**ならずと**おもひ (Printed in full in top margin; readings specified by main text glosses shown in bold)	きみがためにいしやうに**く**んずれとも、きみらんじゃをきゞながら**き**やう**か**うせず**と** (Based on main text glosses)	Though for your sake I perfume my clothes, while you sense orchid and musk you think they are not fragrant. (Ranzan) / Though for your sake I perfume my clothes, while you sense orchid and musk you find them not to be fragrant. (Yamazaki)
Commentary	じやかうのにほひをくんずれともかうばしからずとおもひ		Even when I perfume with the scents of sweet-smelling plants and musk-deer scent, you think they aren't fragrant.

associated with each character – decisions that may reflect slightly different interpretations of meaning or may be mainly stylistic (as in the case of 薫, which is understood as a verb meaning something like 'perfume' in both editions but given its Chinese-style (*onyomi*) reading *kunzu* in one edition and a vernacular (*kunyomi*) reading as *takimono su* in the other). Another level of choices involves dealing with grammatical mismatches between classical Chinese and Japanese that lack a fixed reading convention: 馨香, normally a noun 'fragrance', is used as a verb to mean 'think that (something) is fragrant', a usage that occurs in classical Chinese without any extra grammatical marking[13] but which in Japanese requires specifying different grammatical information. Faced with this structure, the two editions differ on whether to suggest a missing verb indirectly by adding a complementiser (*to*) or to go a step further and add a verb as well ('thinking that' *to omoi*). Tracing the history of earlier glosses to these lines, clusters of more variable readings emerge around these tricky points of interpretation: for example, in a twelfth-century manuscript of the 'New Ballads', multiple glosses are added around 馨香 to reflect one reading with an added verb and one without (Ōta and Kobayashi 1982),[14] and several different possible readings for this phrase can also be found in medieval commentaries to the *Chanting Collection* (Itō et al. 1989). Since nineteenth-century readers inherited the diversity of earlier interpretations along with new debates about language and writing, it comes as no surprise that their culture of kundoku reading was complex and marked by its own factional trends and divisions (Saitō 2014, Ch. 4).

The distributed paratextual mode of translation at work here means that committing to a single interpretation isn't strictly necessary – glosses and commentarial paraphrases can engage with the language of the poem from multiple, even contradictory angles. Rather than replacing the original with a single new version, gloss-based strategies of translation instead overlay one or more additional sets of interpretive information onto a text – which may be aimed at specifying a complete Japanese reading, providing specialised information about 'correct' Chinese-style pronunciation of a phrase, giving synonyms for difficult words or filling in background information or allusions. These various interventions into the reading of a text are so closely interlinked with each other that separating out translation from other kinds of interpretive aids may be counterproductive; we are dealing here with an interpretive system or ecology in which translation is positioned, often invisibly, as one among many interconnected processes of understanding a text.

Translational glosses that begin life as paratext can become text: a kundoku reading might replace a reading more closely patterned on the Chinese text and begin to circulate independently as a substitute, perhaps even evolving away from the original gloss-based style of language to meet different literary needs.[15] However, some approaches to handling texts made a point of keeping glosses closely dependent on the patterns of Chinese-style writing; one attested kind of reading practice particularly associated with poetry and educational primers, known as *monzenyomi* (文選読み '*Wenxuan* reading', after a Six Dynasties literary anthology), involved repeating each line in both Chinese-style pronunciations and a kundoku rendering to firmly link the two together, maintaining the layering practice of the gloss. The system of equivalences established through kundoku reading could also be applied in the opposite direction to create new texts modelled on classical Chinese writing (though still potentially based on Japanese words). Gloss-based approaches to translation thus gave rise to various forms of language – elegant recitation registers rich in Chinese-based words used for public readings of the classics, styles of written Japanese patterned on kundoku language or various forms of more or less orthodox-looking kanbun used to write Japanese by applying kundoku reading strategies in reverse.

The editions introduced in this section suggest some key points about how a fully developed system of kundoku-based 'translation' could shape the reading of Bai Juyi's poetry – the layering potential of a paratextual mode of translation; the way it allowed the task of translation to be distributed across multiple stages of interpretation, styles of spoken and written language, and readers distant in time and space; and the way it could promote the creation of new styles of language to be used more widely. The full history of this approach to dealing with texts is a rich and complex one, in which early modern developments, like the rise of interest in vernacular Chinese and scholarly debates over the practice of kundoku, deserve the attention they have recently been receiving in scholarship, but my focus for the rest of this chapter will be on an earlier period, from the rise of written glosses applied to classical Chinese belletristic texts in the tenth century until the shift to print culture in the sixteenth – a loosely defined medieval stage of Japanese translation in which glossing, commentary, poetic composition and anecdotal storytelling evolved together around certain classical Chinese poems.

Looking for 'translation' in premodern Japan – reflections of 'The Lingyuan Lady'

Just as the fundamental practices of premodern Japanese literacy tend to create multiple distributed, deferred and semi-reversible moments of translation, this is also true as we look more widely at adaptations and retellings in various kinds of Japanese written language. This section will look at the complex translational space that grew up around Bai Juyi's poem 'The Lingyuan Lady', a 'New Ballads' poem about an imperial concubine sent away from court into seclusion in the desolate wilderness setting of the last emperor's mausoleum, and will begin to map some of the different kinds of language that constitute that space. I will focus on the following section, which describes the lonely isolation of the lady exiled to Lingyuan once she has been shut away in the mountains:

松門到曉月徘徊。柏城盡日風蕭瑟。
松門柏城幽閉深。聞蟬聽鸎感光陰。
眼看菊蕊重陽淚。手把梨華寒食心。
手把梨花無人見。綠蕪牆繞青苔院。[16]

Beyond pine gates that meet the dawn, the moon drifts and wanders;
Through cypress walls, all day long the wind whistles and cries.
Pine gate and cypress walls, deep in quiet confinement;
Listening to cicadas, hearing the warbler, she grieves for the fleeting days.
Eyes gaze on chrysanthemums – autumn festival tears;
Hand plucks a pear blossom – thoughts of spring observances.

Layered translations 59

Hand plucks a pear blossom, no one there to see;
Green leaves smother, walls encircle the moss-grown courtyard.

Here I have given just the Chinese characters most likely encountered by Japanese readers – but what about their initial readings in Japanese? Although there is clear evidence for kundoku reading practices from the early stages of Japanese written culture, customs of manuscript glossing developed more slowly and unevenly, so we can only glimpse the first translational readings of these lines in fragmentary quotations scattered through earlier texts. From the mid-Heian period onward, however, developing practices of written glossing meant that certain acts of kundoku reading left increasingly visible traces on manuscripts. In the case of Bai Juyi's 'New Ballads', a substantial set of readings survives in a manuscript from the early twelfth century, known as the Kanda MS *Collected Works of Bai Juyi Vols 3–4*.[17]

I have summarised the Japanese readings suggested in the Kanda MS for this section of 'The Lingyuan Lady', though by necessity this representation simplifies the dense layering of partial information provided. Most of the Japanese particles and inflections that I have specified with modern *katakana* are actually reflected by a system of dots and other small symbols around the characters (*okototen* ヲコト点); character readings are only occasionally spelled out in *kana* (though one character, 院 in the final line, also gets a Chinese-style tone mark), but some compounds are marked to suggest a phonographic or a logographic reading. The result is a set of adjustments to the process of reading the lines as Japanese, which do not quite aim to specify a complete or a singular translation:

松門、暁ニ至テ月＊徘徊ス、
栢城、盡日（ヒネモ（す））ニ、風、蕭瑟タリ、
松門、柏城、幽閉、深シ［クシテ］、
蟬ヲ聞キ、鷺ヲ聴キテ［キテノミ、］光陰ニ感ス、
眼ニ菊蕊ヲ看レハ［ル］、重陽ノ涙＊、
手ニ梨花［華］ヲ把レハ、寒食ノ心＊、
手ニ梨花ヲ把(ト)レトモ、人ノ見ル無シ、
緑蕪ノ牆(カ（き）)、青苔ノ院ヲ繞(メク)レリ、
        (Adapted from Ōta and Kobayashi 1982)

There are several places in this passage (noted with *) where a gloss has been marked with a hook-like symbol indicating it should be disregarded, suggesting either self-correction or a difference of opinion between glossators that nonetheless was preserved visibly on the page. These include a mark suggesting 月 'moon' be followed by the Japanese particle *ni* – i.e., someone thought it should be read *tsuki ni* 'in the moonlight' and then either changed his mind or was overruled by a later hand. This could reflect a difference in interpretation – rather than having the moon wander, it may be easier to imagine the lady wandering in the moonlight – but this reading is unlikely to be adopted by readers familiar with Chinese-style couplets, since it would distort the grammatical parallelism between lines which otherwise match each other closely. The other contested glosses in this section add a verb of existence *ari* after the noun phrases 重陽ノ涙 'autumn festival tears' and 寒食ノ心 'thoughts of spring observances', a question of differing opinions about style (whether it sounds better to make lines of poetry into complete sentences or allow evocative sentence fragments) rather than interpretation of basic meaning.

Glosses provided as alternative readings (shown in square brackets) also reflect some differences of opinion about proper kundoku reading style. In a line like 'Eyes gaze on chrysanthemums – autumn festival tears (眼看菊蕊重陽涙)', should the connection between the two phrases be made clearer or left more ambiguous? The main gloss of 看 as 看レハ suggests a causal or temporal connection, e.g., 'When/as her eyes gaze on chrysanthemums', while the alternative 看ル simply breaks the line into two separate phrases. An alternative gloss adding a restrictive particle *nomi* 'only' after 'Listening to cicadas, hearing the warbler' places a particular emphasis on the loneliness of the lady's dwelling, where nothing but the sounds of birds and insects breaks the deep quiet.

Rather than working as free zones of individual interpretation, layered glosses and commentaries tend to be heavily structured by patterns of educational transmission and sources of social authority, and the Kanda MS is no exception. The compiler Fujiwara no Shigeaki selectively added traditional reading marks from the major scholarly houses (Ōe, Sugawara, Hino Fujiwara and Shigeaki's own Ceremonial-branch Fujiwara), inscribing an overtly multi-voiced and composite set of 'translations' around the poems. Kobayashi Yoshinori's work on glosses to Bai Juyi's 'New Ballads' (in Ōta 1994b), which brings together early written quotations of poetic recitation with evidence from the Kanda MS and another later medieval manuscript that separates readings from different scholarly houses by colour, suggests that the various house reading traditions may have coalesced quite early, by the late tenth century – which is to say, much of the work of linking characters or phrases to Japanese readings had been done by that point – but that a situation of stable competition and selection between reading traditions then persisted for centuries without transitioning to a single standard. However, some medieval glossators, for example monks unaffiliated with any of these scholarly houses, also chose to mix and match readings across lineages or to create new readings themselves. The stability of the reading system around these poems, including the strength of individual translational calques between character and reading, varied between communities – in this sense, their translation was an ongoing process continually being renegotiated, rather than a single discrete act that could be performed once by an individual.[18]

Alternate glosses like these suggest an ongoing effort to refine and prescriptively record an aesthetics of kundoku language, which functioned as a recognisable high-register style adapted to formal writing and recitation. Though kundoku language might be characterised as 'vernacular' in the sense of a local rather than cosmopolitan variety, it certainly isn't 'vernacular' in the sense of everyday or colloquial language. Rather than aiming for transparent communication, a fluent and invisible 'native' style or a conversational tone, it drew explicitly on its associations with Chinese-style writing and with public speech (Steininger 2017, Chapter 5; Saitō 2014: 102–112).

The developing status of kundoku language as an elegant performance register and as a worthy replacement for the highly patterned literary forms of Chinese-style poetry is underscored by the rise of the specialised type of poem-chanting known as *rōei* (朗詠), in which couplets of Chinese-style verse were intoned musically in precisely this style of 'semi-translation'.[19] Premodern Japanese court tales and diaries depict aristocrats performing *rōei* as a kind of allusive punctuation for conversation and a way to lend ceremonial depth to moments of heightened emotion. In the *Tale of Genji* (源氏物語, early eleventh century), phrases from 'The Lingyuan Lady' colour the expressions of a priest counselling a young woman toward a life of religious seclusion:

> 'Life in this realm is like a fragile leaf', he told her. Despite being a priest, he pronounced 'By the pine gates, the moon wanders until dawn . . .' (松門に暁至りて月徘徊す) in a most elegant and impressive manner, and she felt he was speaking of these things in just the way she wished.
>
> The next day, the sound of 'the wind blowing all through the day' (ひねもすに吹く風) was sad and lonely. She heard His Reverence saying, 'Ah, on this kind of day a mountain ascetic will weep!', and thought, 'Now I'm a mountain ascetic too – my endless tears have a reason behind them after all' . . .[20]

The couplet has come unmoored from the original poem and its social-criticism message, being used instead to comment on a voluntary setting of religious seclusion in the deep mountains. At this point in the story, the young woman (known as Ukifune) has fled her past life and is living in hiding at the foot of Mt Hiei, cared for by elderly nuns who still hope to arrange a marriage for her and reintroduce her to the secular world against her will – quiet seclusion is Ukifune's own wish after her traumatic experiences of romance. This passage occurs shortly after an eminent prelate stopping by her retreat has at last yielded to Ukifune's entreaties and helped her become a nun. His words turn the example of the Lingyuan Lady inside out and make her mausoleum a place of peaceful refuge, using her story to underscore the message that acknowledging the misery and transience of life can bring comfort and spiritual growth. Deeply affected by this perspective, Ukifune continues to experience her surroundings through the language of the poem; the lonely wind the following day, which helps her recognise her new status as an ascetic, 'blows all day long' in a description clearly drawing on (a kundoku reading of) Bai Juyi's couplet. Taking on the translated identity of the Lingyuan Lady has allowed her to define and understand her new life as a nun.

The description of the prelate reciting from the poem skilfully 'despite being a priest' reflects the ambiguous status of Bai Juyi's romantic narrative poetry (and perhaps rōei in general) as texts able to find a home in both the university and the court salon, balanced between the dignity of association with Chinese-style textuality and an elegant but slightly frivolous or transgressive air of worldly romance. The image of a venerable priest trying to inspire a vulnerable young woman by teaching her the romantic tragedy of an exiled court lady has a satirical edge – although, as a kind of expedient means, it also has respectable Buddhist precedents. When Ukifune thinks that his words are just the right kind of comfort for her, she is commenting more generally on his sympathetic attitude and the powerful relief of having her wishes for religious escape taken seriously at last – but she may also be grateful that the prelate is making an effort to speak to her in elegant poetry rather than daunting scripture. The social flexibility of poems like 'The Lingyuan Lady', particularly when represented in kundoku readings, made them more accessible for writers without specialised training in Chinese-style scholarship, contributing to the wide scope of their adaptation into various other literary contexts.

At the same time, these wider and more flexible patterns of reception were always linked at some level with developments in Chinese-style composition. In skilled Chinese-style literary writing of the tenth and eleventh centuries, phrases like 'pine gate' 松門 and the close analogue 'pine door' 松戸 were distinctive enough to act as intertextual signs for 'The Lingyuan Lady', but the setting evoked by these phrases was subject to reimagining and interference from other associations.

A pine gate sometimes stands for a mausoleum or context of mourning – though often without the socially critical tone of Bai Juyi's work, which questioned the wastefulness and cruelty of forcing a court lady to live out her life as a designated mourner. In a memorial prayer by Ōe no Mochitoki collected in the *Honchō monzui* (本朝文粋, eleventh century), a 'pine gate' is associated with the grief of the departed man's mother:

堂上有齡傾之老母、泣後事於松門之煙、室中多年少之遺弟、失前途於荊谿之雲。[21]
At the hall is his aged mother – she weeps for his fate in the smoke of the pine gate. In the chamber, his many young brothers – they have lost their way amid the clouds of the thorn-choked valley.[22]

In contrast, two prefaces to poetry gatherings written by the tenth-century scholar/poet Ki no Tadana (紀斉名, 957–999) use 'pine gate/pine door' 松門・松戸 as a positive image for religious seclusion, not necessarily linked to death or mourning – an association that parallels (and may have informed) the *Genji* scene discussed earlier. A preface he composed for a poetry gathering at Zenrinji Temple does mention early on that Zenrinji was founded by a past emperor, perhaps keeping in mind the temple's connection to Emperor Seiwa (清和天皇, 850–880) and the prayer hall built for him there shortly before his death, but his description of a tranquil religious setting where poets can savour the emotional inspirations of autumn 'shaded by pine and cypress' (蔭松柏) and where 'through the pine door visitors are few' (松戸人希) seems to celebrate the air of seclusion rather than responding with loneliness or mourning.[23] Another preface, written for a poetry session linked to lectures on the *Lotus Sutra*, seems to abandon any connection to an imperial tomb and use the 'pine gate' as a symbol of meditative refuge:

松門塵斂、人我之心早銷、苔径煙深、禅定之思弥静。[24]
At the pine gate the dust lies quiet, and one's sense of self and other quickly vanishes; on the mossy path the mist lies thick, and one's inner focus grows calm.

The titles of both pieces situate them in highly social rather than solitary contexts of religious experience, suggesting that the pine-gated retreat has become an idealised image that can be used in conventional praise of a religious setting – even one quite unlike the Lingyuan Lady's mausoleum.

Ki no Tadana was a respected scholar who made his career on his ability to write and teach Chinese-style literature, but his knowledge of 'Chinese' was not general or conversational – if suddenly transported to the Song capital, he would have struggled with spoken communication, though he would have been able to exchange written messages with the highly educated.[25] He was highly skilled, however, at composing in the accepted classical Chinese-style genres of his day, which included adapting the language and imagery of poems like 'The Lingyuan Lady' to generate new phrasings suited to specific set topics and social contexts. This widespread practice of composing in classical Chinese as a written language, without necessarily any knowledge of spoken Chinese, is perhaps a kind of invisible translation – the flip side of the largely invisible oral translations performed in the case of kundoku reading without written glosses – but could also be taken as a reminder that knowledge of a language is not straightforwardly binary but amounts to a variable set of competencies that may be spread differently over various styles of spoken and written language that we bundle together to call 'a language'.[26]

The creative power of gloss-based translation to shape new kinds of writing is illustrated even more clearly by forms of kanji-based, mainly logographic writing that do not adhere consistently to norms of classical Chinese literary style but instead adapt elements of that style to write Japanese. The diary of the celebrated waka poet Fujiwara Teika (藤原定家, 1162–1241) is one such example; its vocabulary and grammatical structures are informed in part by well-known classical Chinese texts used as primers, including Bai Juyi's poetry. In one entry, Teika uses the verb 徘徊 *haikai su* to lend a poetic flavour to a moonlit walk in his garden:

> 庭梅盛開、芬芳四散。家中無人、一身徘徊。
> (Inamura ed. 2002, Jishō 4–2–14, vol. 1 p. 1)

> The plums in the garden were in full bloom, their fragrance spreading in all directions. There was no one else at the house, and I wandered there alone.

徘徊 is not a particularly rare word (it also appears in other famous Bai Juyi poems, for example), but 'The Lingyuan Lady' would have been one well-known source acting to boost familiarity with this kind of literary vocabulary among writers like Teika who were not trained Chinese studies scholars.

Although Teika added no glosses to his text, there can be no doubt that he was writing with Japanese language in mind; the style of inscription incorporates a range of priorities, moving back and forth between fairly orthodox classical Chinese like this and more localised phrases difficult to understand without reading them as Japanese. In this entry, for example, his poetic enjoyment of the garden is interrupted by news of a disastrous fire sweeping through the capital, and he notes that his father takes refuge with a son-in-law nearby: 'he went across to Lord Shigezane's house in Kitakōji' (渡北小路成実朝臣宅給). The final character 給 is customarily used to write the common classical Japanese honorific *-tamau*, which follows a verb to show respect for its subject; not only does this honorific demand a

Japanese reading, but since it should directly follow the main verb, its position at the end of the sentence assumes that the verb 渡 will be read after its object in Japanese word order. This kind of kundoku-based logographic written Japanese was widespread across many practical, official and belletristic genres and could also mix with more phonographic modes of writing, so that it becomes necessary to describe premodern Japanese writing along axes of linguistic style and script rather than defining a single point where Chinese writing becomes Japanese.

Productive translational mixing of poetic vocabulary, topics and imagery also occurred in the realm of waka poetry, though directed in a more focussed way through genre-appropriate channels. This brief thirty-one syllable verse form, which played a key role as social and occasional poetry in the Heian court, was generally written in a kana-dominated phonographic style and relied on a restricted and lyrically resonant set of Japanese vocabulary that gained power from intertextual allusion. In this context, 'The Lingyuan Lady' served as a topic for allusive variation (本説 *honzetsu*) linked to the developing poetics of reclusion. As in some of the Chinese-style poetry previously discussed, the phrase 'pine gate' 松の戸, with its allusive echoes of Bai Juyi's lines, became a poetic keyword for a hermit's mountain retreat; for example, in the following influential verse by Princess Shokushi (式子内親王, c. 1149–1201), where no one but the dripping snowmelt comes to knock at her gate:

On the occasion of offering up a hundred-poem sequence, a spring poem (Princess Shokushi 式子内親王):

山ふかみ春ともしらぬ松のとにたえだえかかる雪の玉水[27]
So deep in the mountains – as I wait unaware of the coming spring, they knock fitfully at my pine gate: drops of melting snow.

The phrase *matsu no to* 'pine gate' gains an irresistible double meaning in Japanese, which fits the theme of a solitary speaker waiting and hoping for a visitor: *matsu* can mean 'pine tree' or the verb 'to wait', allowing it to form part of two overlapping phrases within the poem. Reading this poem in the voice of the Lingyuan Lady is not made strictly necessary by the unambiguous use of intertextual clues – but the possibility is created by the distinctive 'pine gate' and the context of mountain seclusion. The drops of melting snow that first bring news of spring also echo the seasonal voices of cicada and warbler that reached the Lingyuan Lady as her sole messages from the outside world.

A quick glance across a wider sample of Chinese-style poems and waka suggests several approaches to using Bai Juyi's works as a prompt or inspiration for new poetry. To begin with, there is the practice of taking a line or couplet of Bai Juyi's as the topic for a new verse, which would systematically reuse that line's vocabulary or established synonyms and allusive key words. In this category are topic-line poems in both Chinese-style and waka forms (*kudaishi* 句題詩 and *kudai waka* 句題和歌).[28] In a somewhat more flexible mode of adaptation, there are examples that take more general inspiration from one of Bai Juyi's poems as a whole (or treat the idea of the whole poem as a set topic). The following verse was apparently composed at a gathering where poets were issued poems from Bai Juyi's 'New Ballads' as challenge topics for waka:

> When composing waka with topics from the 'New Ballads' (楽府を題にて), on the idea (心) of the Lingyuan Lady (Minamoto no Mitsuyuki 源光行):
>
> とぢはつるみ山のおくの松の戸をうらやましくもいづる月かな[29]
>
> Waiting shut away in the deep mountains – through a pine gate, how I envy the emerging moon.

This poem selects certain elements of Bai Juyi's lines to follow closely (the key images of the pine gate and moon), as well as defining and adapting an overall atmosphere for the poem (loneliness, trapped claustrophobia, an isolated mountain setting). At the same time, recreating something of the poem in the compact and distinctive form of a waka entails highlighting a particular perspective on the material – in this case, suggesting a hint of yearning for religious awakening in the form of the emerging moon, often linked to enlightenment in the language of waka.

These approaches generally have in common the refinement of key words or images that help identify Bai Juyi's verse as the ground for allusive variation. For example, the topically arranged *Fuboku wakashō* (夫木和歌抄, fourteenth century) has a section of poems on 'Chinese ladies', in which the Lingyuan Lady has her own category, gathering several waka interpretations of the story; all make use of a secluded mountain setting and either a pine gate or the tear-like dew on a chrysanthemum as elements defining the intertextual signature of Bai Juyi's poem.[30] As 'The Lingyuan Lady' became codified as part of the language of waka poetry, 'translating' it into waka form became a matter of using a discrete set of intertextual cues.

Retelling the story of the Lingyuan Lady in detail would be both impossible and unnecessary in a waka poem, but prose tales give space to experiment with more expansive modes of adaptation. The collection *Tales of China* (*Kara monogatari* 唐物語, probably twelfth century)[31] is sometimes talked about under the heading of 'translated anecdotes' (*honyaku setsuwa* 翻訳説話, a modern term), but its free adaptations into the genre of the courtly poem-tale show different priorities from the close coordination of a kundoku reading or the keyword-based allusive reworking of a waka poem. The story about the Lingyuan Lady found in this collection is framed as a retelling for new audiences, opening with the general introduction 'Long ago, there was someone who was shut away within a palace called Lingyuan . . .' (昔陵園といふ宮のうちにとぢこめられたる人ありけり). After expanding in the conventional language of romantic tales on the lady's superlative beauty and how she was slandered at court by jealous competitors, it reimagines the lyrical scene of her mountain seclusion with new seasonal imagery and a selective approach to key plot points and phrases. Despite its growing resonance in waka poetry, 'pine gate' doesn't appear at all here. In place of the pine and cypress (lacking strong seasonal associations), there is a new set-piece following lonely life at the mausoleum through the seasons from spring to autumn and culminating with a waka poem:

> Most days she spent in loneliness within this secluded palace, and in response to the sound of the wind and the cries of the insects (風のをとむしのねにつけても) she suffered every possible feeling. While she lived this way, at long last it became spring; even as the land softened, with mists trailing from the mountainsides all around and bracken shoots in the meadows sprouting forth in the morning rain, she felt envious yearning on her own account. As the fragrance of blossoms filled the air, her heart was troubled in her solitary bed, and though all that entered at her window was the misty spring moon that added to her grief, its light lay faintly and made no reply to her entreaties. While she spent her days like this, spring passed and summer reached its height, and at last the waning days of autumn returned. She saw that the white chrysanthemums, which bloomed in such profusion, were wet with evening dew; she thought of that celebration in the past known as the Chongyang banquet (むかしの重陽の宴といひし事思いでられて),[32] and it grew still harder to hold back her tears.
>
> みるたびも涙つゆけきしらぎくの花もむかしやこひしかるらん
> With every glance, tears dropping like dew; white chrysanthemums – do they long for days past?[33]

As Komine Kazuaki (2006) has pointed out, this passage owes a great deal to tale literature and the language of waka poetry.[34] The lady's emotional response to the sounds of nature closely mirrors that of the grieving emperor in the opening chapter of the *Tale of Genji*, who finds after the death of Genji's mother that 'in response to the sound of the wind and the cries of the insects', (風の音、虫の音につけて) he feels nothing but sorrow.[35] The seasonal descriptions that follow replace most of the details of Bai Juyi's poem with new imagery; trailing mists (霞), bracken shoots (野辺の早蕨), and the misty spring moon (朧月夜) are all recognisable spring topics in waka poetry, common enough that they cannot be pinpointed as specific allusions but instead give a more general sense that the story has been translated into the familiar language of waka. The key image remaining from Bai Juyi's poem is the chrysanthemum, a poetic topic that fits naturally into the world of waka and was already being used in some poems on 'The Lingyuan Lady'. The kind of translation or adaptation happening in this text is far from a straightforward transfer of meaning from source text to target language – it involves a rich network of other literary associations and intertexts that also help constitute the target language.

A full history of all the texts and practices involved in the reception of even this single Chinese poem would be beyond the scope of this chapter, but these few examples show a wide range of possible texts we might consider as early Japanese translations of Bai Juyi's poetry – including closely bound paratextual glosses (which can also reflect or generate possible stand-alone translations in speech or writing); allusive developments that selectively incorporate parts of the poem within Chinese-style and vernacular genres; and loose retellings of the story behind the poem, mediated by other literary tropes. In the course of these engagements, some kind of communication from classical Chinese to Japanese seems to have occurred – but thanks to the pre-prepared calquing system of kundoku reading and the gradual filtering of poetry through multiple different kinds of written language, it's not easy to say exactly where. Rather than trying to isolate a single moment of transfer between two discrete languages, understanding the reception of classical Chinese texts requires us to look at multiple moments of 'translation' between modes (speech/writing), styles/registers or genres (waka, kanshi) of language.[36] Some of these translational practices are based on a logic of supplementary glossing rather than rewriting or replacement, though glosses always carry the potential to be used later as a stand-in for the source text (and can more easily carry something of the source text across boundaries of language and written style). Many of these practices are also collaborative and widely distributed across multiple 'translators', with individual decisions about cross-linguistic equivalence hidden between the lines and in the invisible spaces between writing and speech.

Thinking about translation and premodern Japan, then and now

Medieval writers working with classical Chinese poetry did not position themselves as 'translators' in the sense of adopting a distinct intellectual identity defined by its involvement with classical Chinese and shared across all such writers. Perhaps due in part to the stepwise and distributed nature of translation across lines of spoken and written linguistic style, the roles of translators and the progression of translation itself are often invisible or at least anonymous. Exceptions tend to involve translators who claim another valued literary identity, either as a poet or as a scholar (a lecturer or author of commentary).

Even here, the dynamics around authorship and ownership of 'translations' can be complex. For example, some glossed manuscripts and commentaries have colophons aiming at a personal and literary tone (e.g., Shigeaki's for the Kanda-bon), but others are minimal, mentioning the copiers and glossators briefly if at all; many medieval commentaries on the *Japanese and Chinese-style Chanting Collection* (some of which develop vernacular explanations of lines from Bai Juyi's poetry) are anonymous products of multiple commentators working in a temple-based educational setting. Commentary was a widespread and multi-faceted social practice that could function as high-status scholarly work or an anonymous aide to basic education, depending on the intended audience.

Medieval writers also described their translational interactions with classical Chinese texts in a variety of ways. Verbs simply meaning something like 'to read' (よむ) are common. There are also specific terms for recitation (e.g. ながむ, 朗詠す); for adding glosses (e.g. 点す 'mark' or 'point', used even when the glosses involve kana); for converting between kanji-heavy and kana-heavy styles of writing (e.g., 和らぐ); and for poetic composition based on classical Chinese texts (e.g., using something as a topic (題) or conveying the essence (心) of another work in waka form). The language of premodern Japanese translation highlights different sets of meaningful dividing lines across the spectrum of linguistic variety, structuring the conceptual space surrounding texts brought from the continent in terms of differences in script or style of language, conversion between writing and speech or exchanges of meaning and diction between closely prescribed poetic forms – not on transfer of meaning between two languages.

Even when a contrast is drawn for specific rhetorical purposes between 本朝 'our court' and 異朝 'that other court' (usually China or other states on the continent), the focus tends to be on similarities and differences in custom or precedent rather than straightforwardly defined linguistic difference. This point is vividly illustrated by a widely circulated fantasy of poetic translation that appears in the Heian travel narrative *Tosa nikki* (土佐日記, Tosa Diary). It tells how at the end of a long stay in Tang China, the diplomat Abe no Nakamaro composed a waka poem on the rising moon at his farewell banquet, reflecting his longing for his homeland; he writes out a kind of summary or simulation of his waka in 'men's characters' (kanji) and then explains it in detail to someone who understands Japanese:

> One might think the people of that country (かの国人) would not be able to listen and understand the poem, but he took the meaning of its words and gave an outline in men's characters (言の心を、男文字に様を書き出だして), and when he explained it to someone conversant with our language (ここの言葉伝へたる人), they must have caught its meaning, for they praised it quite beyond anyone's expectation. Though between China and this land the language differs (言異なる), the light of the moon must be the same, and so surely people's hearts (心) are the same as well?[37]

As it is set in China and involves non-Japanese speakers, this episode might seem like an obvious place to highlight linguistic difference, but it does not present a clear binary contrast between Chinese and Japanese languages with their own spoken and written forms. Instead translation is imagined as a combination of kundoku-based written composition (writing in Chinese characters by applying the translational calques developed through kundoku reading in reverse) and spoken interpretation in Japanese, which are together used to confirm a shared poetic sensibility transcending language. The roles of several different spoken and written styles of language within this imagined system of translation are clearly delimited, without assuming that speech and writing 'in Chinese' must be firmly linked together. As Ross King (2015: 12–13) has noted, while movements to bring spoken and written language closer together played a central role in the creation of 'linguistic and literary modernity' in Japan, Korea and China, premodern East Asia was shaped by an ideology of 'mismatch between speech and writing' (言文不一致).[38]

In this sense, given the realities of premodern Japanese literacies and literary genres, conceptualising 'translation' meant taking a stance toward the gap between spoken language and various genres of writing, either protecting and valuing that gap or trying to conceal it. The interpreter in Nakamaro's story is an anonymous cipher, and the narrator doesn't bother to tell us whether he ever explained the poem in Chinese or what that translation was like – the form and meaning of the poem remain firmly Nakamaro's, and the story comes close to making spoken Chinese invisible. It is not uncommon for medieval scenarios of imagined translation to at least partially obscure the existence of Chinese as a spoken language, pointing toward a binary model of Chinese=writing/Japanese=speech or at least to a fantasy of Chinese characters as universally readable without need for translation (or the creation of new localised character-word links) at any stage. But this idea clashes with reality in various ways – in the diversity of distinct styles of written Japanese that do not transparently reflect speech and in the persistence of interest in Chinese-style readings and pronunciations, even if not in conversational spoken language.

This problem of how speech and writing should figure in the handling of Chinese poetry could be approached in other ways, for example by echoing traditions about the collaborative chain translation practiced on sutras in medieval China. One monastic commentary on the *Japanese and Chinese-style Chanting Collection* (和漢朗詠集) opens by explaining the 'Wa 和' of the anthology's title, identifying 大和 as a name for Japan and inventing an etymology: when sutras were being transmitted, Sanskrit language was 'softened' or 'gentled' (和(やわ)らぐ) into Chinese, and Chinese language then 'gentled' into the language of 'our court', so Japan itself came to be known as 大和国 'the land of great gentling'. This impression of stepwise sutra translation is then expanded to apply to poetry:

> India (language), known as Sanskrit, is not only harsh but difficult to hear and understand (強キノミニモアラス、其聞トヲシ). This must mean things like *dharani*. Chinese language means today's Chinese-style poetry (詩賦) and so forth. The speech of China (漢土ノ言) is still difficult to understand, so again in this country it has been gentled (此国ニ和ケタリ). Thus it is soft to speak and easy to listen to (言モヤワラカニ、聞モヤスシ). This means things like today's thirty-one character waka poem.[39]

Sanskrit, Chinese and Japanese languages are distinguished on aesthetic grounds ('strong/harsh' or 'soft/gentle') as kinds of speech suitable for reciting different kinds of poetry in order to fit an underlying 'Three Realms' cosmology of evolution from India to China to Japan – a process of stepwise translation that might be applied to specific texts like sutras or to languages as a whole and that results in parallel coordinated genres of 'poetry'. At the same time, the entire logic of the passage depends on writing: the character 和 is used to write both Yamato 大和, one name for the Japanese state, and the verb *yawaragu* 和 'to soften', although these two words are linguistically unrelated.

This idea of waka poetry as the end result of a 'softening' or 'harmonizing' aesthetic process applied to Chinese poetry and ultimately sutras also appears in the fifteenth-century Noh play *Haku Rakuten* (白楽天), in which Bai Juyi visits Japan only to be bested in a poetic contest by a humble Japanese fisherman (actually the Sumiyoshi deity in disguise).[40] The play takes Nakamaro's translation fantasy to a logical extreme, as any language barriers between Bai Juyi and the fisherman are entirely invisible, leaving only a carefully staged debate over the aesthetics of different poetic genres in which the waka can emerge as superior. The fisherman responds to Bai Juyi's classical Chinese couplet by instantly 'translating' it into the form of a waka – a feat of poetic skill that forces the Tang poet to retreat, allegedly wishing he could compose waka himself. In a further ironic twist, the Chinese-style couplet Bai Juyi composes in the play, although widely attributed to him in late medieval Japan, seems in fact to be the work of an eighth-century Japanese poet. These two fantasies of translation – Nakamaro's waka written in Chinese characters and the Sumiyoshi fisherman's one-upping adaptation of Bai Juyi's verse – share a strong drive to connect and contrast different styles of poetic practice and a comparative indifference to constructing national languages and their borders.

A search for premodern Japanese translation leaves us with many examples that do not replace the original but instead distribute its interpretation across a more finely grained set of linguistic distinctions using an open-ended set of layered glosses, paraphrases and commentarial explanations. Translation is sometimes described as creating an intermediate 'third language' – but the reality can be even more complex, with the formation of innumerable fragmented intermediate languages that split off and blend into the multiple varieties of written and spoken language already distinguished by the translating community, or trigger the redrawing of new conceptual lines distinguishing language styles. As well as these difficulties defining its start and end points, translation as a process can itself involve other texts, visual configurations and linguistic styles in catalytic roles. Compared to the kind of translation that can be modelled as replacement of an original text in a different language, these approaches make a different range of interpretive decisions and engagements visible. They also highlight some shared issues in thinking about translation of various kinds – particularly the unsustainable fixed and bounded concept of 'a language' that tends to underpin the idea of translation from a source to a target language. Paratextual processes of gloss- and commentary-based translation can create multi-layered texts that resist simple answers to questions like 'what language is it in?', drawing attention to collaborative aspects of translation and the way that it can work in tandem with changes within a language – as well as productively blurring the lines between translation, interpretive glossing and general literacy.

In this sense, premodern Japanese translation as a case study underscores the need for models of language competence and literacy that can describe various combinations of oral and written skills across a spectrum of linguistic styles and can help us move beyond reductive questions like whether Heian aristocrats 'knew Chinese'. Recent work in translation studies, as well as in literacy studies and the sociolinguistics of writing, has been gradually moving away

Layered translations 73

from assuming monolingualism as the norm, instead pioneering an approach to texts as fluid combinations of codes created through sets of practices and strategies for the collaborative negotiation of meaning, and this kind of approach seems like a good fit for the complex translingual spaces of premodern Japan.[41] A translingual approach could free us to better understand how speakers and writers made use of their particular array of linguistic resources in particular settings and to more clearly map the variety of script and language styles distinguished within the interaction between classical Chinese and Japanese texts.

This chapter is only a first exploratory look at how premodern Japanese reception of Bai Juyi's poetry might appear through a translational lens, and there are many more possible texts and angles to consider. Even this preliminary sketch, though, suggests striking patterns of visibility and invisibility on multiple levels. Gloss-based strategies in premodern Japanese translation make a different range of linguistic choices and connections visible and also highlight the range of intertextually complex relationships between 'replacement' translations and the original text. At a more abstract level, thinking about premodern Japanese translation in a flexible and inclusive way that can encompass gloss-based strategies may prompt us to give further thought to certain aspects of translation – intertextuality and the formation of translational equivalences, collaborative distribution, overlap with interpretive commentary – that might be less clearly visible within other systems of language and writing.

Notes

1 Rebekah Clements (2015: 11) notes that 'there was simply no one term that corresponds to a sweeping category of "translation" as we know it in English' and discusses a wide range of early modern terms. See also Wakabayashi 2009 on selected premodern terms viewed through an etymological lens, though I have chosen not to adopt her new category of 'J-translation' out of concern that essentialising the Japanese nature of these practices might further obscure parallels and connections with translation elsewhere in the premodern world.
2 On similar practices of literacy throughout East Asia and beyond, see Kornicki (2018), King (2015), Lurie (2011), and Whitman (2011). There is a recent trend toward using unified English terminology to talk about similar premodern literacy practices, for example 'vernacular reading' in place of Japanese *kundoku* / Chinese *xundu*; this has compelling advantages for promoting cross-linguistic and interdisciplinary work and avoiding nationalistic assumptions, but since the term 'vernacular' is somewhat overdetermined and may confuse discussion of the varied social roles of Japanese language styles, I will keep the romanised term kundoku in this case (see Whitman et al. 2010; Shirane 2014; Kornicki 2018 for helpful discussion).
3 *Hon'yaku* is currently the default translation for English 'translation' and generally shares its conceptual associations, but it still tends to be narrower in usage – for example, the modern Japanese translation found in the margin of many Japanese

editions of classical texts is known as a *gendaigo yaku* 現代語訳 rather than a *hon'yaku* (Emmerich 2013, p. 10). This may have strengthened Saitō's sense of a distinction between translation and commentarial gloss, although the question of whether and how to relate translation and interpretation is one with wide currency (Reynolds 2011, Ch. 8).

4 See Lurie (2011: 323–334) for a critique of this 'bilingual fallacy'. As well as oversimplifying the variety of language styles and their relationships, thinking in terms of Chinese/Japanese bilingualism makes invisible the crucial role played by immigrants from the Korean peninsula in the early development of literacy in Japan.

5 Lurie (2011) examines how a kundoku-based translationese or 'calcolect' generated stylistic varieties of written language in early Japan; Levy (2011: 3) describes kundoku as creating a mediating 'third language' (in Yanabu Akira's sense) that shaped the modern history of translation in Japan; Clements (2015) addresses it both as a form of highly bound translation and as a reading method that creates a kind of translationese; in a recent general introduction to translation, Reynolds (2016) mentions kundoku as a kind of translational 'no-man's land that readers of one language can enter to make sense of writing in another'. Takatsu Takashi (in Nakamura, 2014) has gone a step further and suggested that kundoku readings are a type of contact language (distinct from but parallel to pidgins and creoles).

6 Gerard Genette (1997)'s original definition of the paratext focuses on elements added by the author of the principal text or at least with authorial approval; see Batchelor (2018) for discussion of how this idea has been modified for use in translation studies. I am using the term in a similar sense to Batchelor's: 'a consciously crafted threshold for a text which has the potential to influence the way(s) in which the text is received' (p. 142). See Blom (2017: 9–16) for helpful discussion of glosses as paratexts.

7 This first documented arrival of Bai Juyi's poetry was in 838 CE, though the phrasing of some earlier poetry by Emperor Saga may show exposure to Bai Juyi's work (Shizunaga 2010: 51–64; Smits 1997: 169–171).

8 Ōta et al. (1993) (Taniguchi Kōsuke and Ōsone Shōsuke chapters).

9 Takai Ranzan 高井蘭山 (1762–1838) was known as a writer of popular prose (*gesaku*, *yomihon*) as well as educational works.

10 Yamazaki Kyūsaku 山崎久作 (1796–1856), also known as Yamazaki Yoshinari or Yoshishige, was a kokugaku scholar and member of Takizawa Bakin's literary circle.

11 Saitō (2014: 178–179) discusses the relationship between *kundokutai* as a productive form of language and *kundokubun* as a written transcript of kundoku reading applied to a specific phrase, as well as the variety of terms used in the nineteenth century for both of these concepts (*kundokubun* is often described with terms like *yaku* 訳 or *kai* 解).

12 Ranzan's edition follows a format similar to that of a series of highly successful editions of the Chinese classics, *Plenty of Teachers for the Classics* (*Keiten Yoshi* 経典余師, published widely from 1786–1843). See Suzuki (2007: 145–244) for more detail on *Keiten yoshi* and its implications for literacy, especially p. 198–208 on Ranzan's adoption of the format for primer-like texts.

13 See Zádrapa (2011) on verbal usage of nouns in classical Chinese.

14 The alternative glosses reflect the readings *sezu* and *sezu to omoeri* (the same verb of thinking, marked as stative); the Middle Chinese tone of 罄 is also

Layered translations 75

marked, showing the heterogenous nature of the reading practice represented here. For more on this manuscript (known as the Kanda MS) and its glosses, see the following section.

15 The idea of translation as replacement or rewriting has a well-established history, and Michael Emmerich (2013) has recently built on this by using a broader and more materially grounded idea of 'replacement' in place of the concept of literary reception. Even editions based on paratextual glossing and commentary can be considered replacements in Emmerich's sense – they circulate in place of, while helping to constitute, a notional 'original text'. At this level, an edition with kundoku annotation and a stand-alone translated edition of a text simply adopt different strategies of replacement, with the gloss-based approach making a more direct and visible attempt to evoke an original text.

16 Text adapted slightly from the Kanda MS (Ōta and Kobayashi 1982). There are two substantive differences from the Nawa edition now taken as standard, which has 'swallow' 燕 instead of 'oriole/warbler' 鶯 in the fourth line and 'Plucking a flower, hiding tears' 把花掩涙 in place of the repeated 'Hand plucks a pear blossom' in the seventh line (Zhu 1988). All English translations are my own unless noted otherwise.

17 白氏文集巻第三・巻第四（神田喜一郎旧蔵), reproduced and annotated in Ōta and Kobayashi (1982). According to the colophon, the text of the poems was copied in 1107 CE and the reading marks added later in 1113.

18 As well as in glossed manuscripts used for lectures and other educational purposes, readings of Chinese-style poetry were continually being explored and redefined in commentary. In the case of the 'New Ballads', a few medieval commentaries survive: the twelfth-century *Shin gafu ryakui* 新楽府略意 entry for this section of the poem gives definitions for 光陰 and for the autumn and spring festivals mentioned in the poem, while the thirteenth-century Shinpukuji MS *Shin gafu chū* 新楽府注 echoes the emphasis of some alternate glosses by explaining that since the lady is confined indoors, she must rely on sounds and indirect glimpses of nature to gauge the passage of time (Ōta 1967, 1968). See Shirane (2014) on the role of commentary in mediating translation from classical Chinese to 'high (Heian)' vernacular Japanese, as well as in the early modern rise of intralingual translations from Heian Japanese to contemporary language.

19 On references to *rōei* in premodern texts and the development of a standardised repertoire of couplets and melody patterns over the course of the late Heian period, see Aoyagi (1999). The anthology *Wakan rōeishū*, mentioned earlier, was (among other educational and literary roles) an important collection of material used in this kind of poem-chanting.

20 Abe et al. (1994). Tamagami Takuya (1968: 502) points out that the 'pine gate' quotation from 'The Lingyuan Lady' varies across manuscripts of *The Tale of Genji*; in fact, several texts have *tsuki ni haikai su*, echoing the crossed-out alternate gloss in the Kanda MS discussed earlier, and one seventeenth-century print edition claims this is a reading passed down in the Sugawara scholarly house. Kobayashi Yoshinori (in Ōta 1994b: 268) has also noted the likelihood that Murasaki Shikibu knew Sugawara house readings through her father. For detailed comparative discussion of variants, see Tsukishima (1965: 796–798).

21 Ōsone et al. (1992) (*Honchō monzui* 426, 'Prayer for the forty-ninth day memorial service of Prelate Kaku'un' 為覚運僧都四十九日願文). The celebrated Tendai cleric Kaku'un died in 1007. See also Steininger (2017: 183–184), for discussion of a prayer written on behalf of Fujiwara no Tadahira to commemorate

a temple donation he made in memory of the late emperor (933), which uses 'color of the pines and cypresses' (松柏之色) as reference to an imperial mausoleum while ignoring the inauspicious critical context in Bai Juyi's poem. The evergreen trees 'pine and cypress' have a range of possible intertextual associations and can also stand for enduring virtue.

22 By analogy to 荊溪, the name of an influential Tiantai leader, this image suggests the Tendai Buddhist complex of Mt Hiei.

23 Ōsone et al.. (1992) (*Honchō monzui* 283, 'Seven-character verses on seeing the views at Zenrinji Temple in late autumn' 七言晩秋於禅林寺上方眺望). This line is also included in the 'Mountain Temple' section of the *New Chanting Collection* (*Shinsen rōeishū* 新撰朗詠集, early twelfth century), which suggests its popularity as chanting material and would have further boosted its circulation.

24 Ōsone et al. (1992) (*Honchō monzui* 278, 'Seven-character verses, in late spring when the Assembly for the Promotion of Learning heard a lecture on the Lotus Sutra and together composed on the topic "Focusing one's thoughts in the mountain forest"' 七言暮春勧学会聴講法華経同賦摂念山林).

25 On the limited early history of spoken Chinese teaching in Japan, see Yuzawa (2001). On the practice of communicating in writing known as 'brush talk' (筆談 *hitsudan*), see Kornicki (2018: 100–102).

26 As Steininger (2017: 213) puts it, 'Heian writing in literary Sinitic presents us with a paradox: on the one hand *kundoku* recitation practices firmly seat the production and reception of this literature in a Japanese language environment – in certain respects, this work is just as "vernacular" as the *Tale of Genji* and other works based on *kana* inscription. But at the same time, the *bunshō* aesthetic of Heian poetry and parallel prose is defined through its rejection of the registers of ordinary speech'.

27 The poem was first composed in 1200 for a hundred-poem sequence commissioned by the retired emperor and then included near the beginning of the spring section of the *Shin kokin wakashū* (新古今和歌集 3, Minemura 1995: 23). See also Rasplica Rodd (2015): 'So deep the mountains / waiting unaware that spring / has come sporadic / taps on my pine bough door are / jeweled drops of melting snow'.

28 On topic-line poetry, see Steininger (2017) and Denecke (2007); on kudai waka and translation, see Clements (2015: 103–104).

29 *Shin chokusen wakashū* 1091 (*Shinpen kokka taikan*). Along with the pun on *matsu* (pine/wait for), there is a pun on *urayama* (deep mountains) and *urayamashi* (envious).

30 See 夫木和歌抄 (静嘉堂文庫蔵本), poems 16789–92 (*Shinpen kokka taikan*). The *Shin chokusen wakashū* poem just mentioned appears in this collection as well.

31 The authorship and history of the collection are uncertain, but one theory is that it was compiled by Fujiwara no Shigenori (藤原成範, 1135–87), possibly based on earlier illustrated scrolls of Chinese tales (Geddes 1984).

32 The 'Double Yang' or 'Double Ninth' (重陽) Festival was celebrated on the ninth day of the ninth lunar month and associated with chrysanthemums; my translation of 'The Lingyuan Lady' above renders it more generally as 'autumn festival'. Unlike the other observance mentioned in the poem (the Hanshi or Cold Food Festival in spring), chrysanthemum banquets were customary in the Heian court.

33 Text adapted slightly from the late Kamakura period Sonkeikaku bunko MS transcribed in Ikeda (1972). See also Kobayashi (1998) and Geddes (1984).

34 See also Ikeda (1974: 107–110) on the tendency in *Kara monogatari* to render Bai Juyi's material more courtly (王朝化) by adopting the language of waka and monogatari.
35 *Genji monogatari*, Abe et al.. (1994, vol. 1: 35). In the *Tale of Genji*, the phrase immediately follows a scene in which the emperor tries to console himself with quotations from an even more well-known narrative poem by Bai Juyi, the 'Song of Lasting Sorrow' (長恨歌); in this sense, rewriting Bai Juyi's other poetry in terms of this iconic chapter of the *Tale of Genji* is a step within an even more complex cycle of adaptation and remixing.
36 This layering of interpretations has implications for how we think about the reception of Chinese texts more broadly; Steininger (2016: 126) notes that the academy-based literacies were heavily mediated by 'layers of imported commentary, *kundoku*-based translation, and transmitted vernacular explications. Each time we seem to get close to the "classic", another hermeneutic step intervenes'.
37 *Tosa nikki*, Kikuchi et al. (1995: 17). Lurie (2011: 327–329) describes the scene as a 'complex act of translation' in which the act of summarising a waka poem logographically in Chinese characters creates something a Japanese audience can experience as a Japanese 'paraphrase', while to the Chinese audience it serves as a translation, concluding that 'Premodern sources show tremendous stylistic variety, and sophisticated awareness of that variety on the part of readers and writers, but little to no sign that Chinese-style logographic writing was taken to be *linguistically* separate from phonographically written vernacular styles'. See also Sakaki (2006) and Yoda (2004) for analysis of this story in terms of complex and non-binary comparisons between 'Chinese' and 'Japanese'; Heldt (2005) situates it helpfully within a full discussion of attitudes about language and writing in *Tosa nikki*.
38 As King points out, this term does not describe a situation of diglossia but of (in a translation he provides half-playfully) 'schizoglossographia'.
39 Shoryōbu MS *Rōeishō*, in Itō et al. (1989, vol. 2 ge: 317).
40 See Klein (2013); similar claims about the language of waka appear in medieval commentaries to the first imperial waka anthology (e.g., *Kokin wakashū jo kikigaki sanryūshō*) and seem to have spread widely through various contexts of commentary and storytelling by the late medieval era. See also discussion in Yip (2016: 134–139).
41 See for example Canagarajah (2013) and Lillis (2013). 'Translingual practice' as a key word has been occasionally used in East Asian studies for decades, thanks to Lydia Liu's work, though it has seldom been applied in premodern contexts.

Bibliography

Abe Akio, eds. 1994. *Genji monogatari* (Shinpen nihon koten bungaku zenshū 20–25). Tokyo: Shōgakukan.
Aoyagi Takashi. 1999. *Nihon rōeishi*. Tokyo: Chikuma shoin.
Batchelor, Kathryn. 2018. *Translation and Paratexts* (Translation Theories Explored). London: Routledge.
Blom, Alderik H. 2017. *Glossing the Psalms: The Emergence of the Written Vernaculars in Western Europe from the Seventh to the Twelfth Centuries*. Berlin: De Gruyter.

Canagarajah, A. Suresh. 2013. *Translingual Practice: Global Englishes and Cosmopolitan Relations*. Abingdon: Routledge.
Clements, Rebekah. 2015. *A Cultural History of Translation in Early Modern Japan*. Cambridge: Cambridge University Press.
Denecke, Wiebke. 2007. '"Topic Poetry Is All Ours": Poetic Composition on Chinese Lines in Early Heian Japan'. *Harvard Journal of Asiatic Studies* 67 (1): 1–49.
Emmerich, Michael. 2013. *The Tale of Genji: Translation, Canonization, and World Literature*. New York: Columbia University Press.
Geddes, Ward. 1984. *Kara Monogatari: Tales of China*. Tempe, Arizona: Center for Asian Studies, Arizona State University.
Genette, Gérard. 1997. *Paratexts: Thresholds of Interpretation*. Translated by Jane E. Lewin. Cambridge: Cambridge University Press.
Heldt, Gustav. 2005. 'Writing Like a Man: Poetic Literacy, Textual Property, and Gender in the "Tosa Diary"'. *The Journal of Asian Studies* 64 (1): 7–34.
Ikeda Toshio, ed. 1972. *Kara monogatari: Sonkeikaku bunkobon* (Koten bunko 300). Tokyo: Koten bunko.
Ikeda Toshio. 1974. *Nitchū hikaku bungaku no kiso kenkyū: hon'yaku setsuwa to sono tenkyo*. Tokyo: Kasama shoin.
Inamura Eiichi, ed. 2002. *Kunchū meigetsuki*. Matsue: Matsue Imai shoten.
Itō Masayoshi, Kuroda Akira, and Miki Masahiro, eds. 1989. *Wa-kan rōeishū kochūshaku shūsei*. Kyoto: Daigakudō shoten.
Kikuchi Yasuhiko, Tsurayuki Ki, Michitsuna no Haha, Masanori Kimura, and Tsunehisa Imuta. eds. 1995. *Tosa nikki* (Shinpen nihon koten bungaku zenshū 13). Tokyo: Shōgakukan.
King, Ross. 2015. 'Ditching "Diglossia": Ecologies of the Spoken and Inscribed in Pre-Modern Korea'. *Sunkyun Journal of East Asian Studies* 15 (1).
Klein, Susan. 2013. 'Haku Rakuten'. In *Like Clouds and Mists: Studies and Translations of Nō Plays of the Genpei War*, ed. Elizabeth Oyler and Michael Geoffrey Watson. Ithaca, NY: East Asia Program, Cornell University.
Kō Ranzan. 1835 (orig. preface 1803). *Wakan rōei kokujishō* 和漢朗詠国字抄. 4 vols. Edo: Mankyūdō.
Kobayashi Yasuharu, ed. 1998. *Kara monogatari zenshaku* (Kasama chūshaku sōkan 26). Tokyo: Kasama shoin.
Komine Kazuaki. 2006. *Inseiki bungakuron*. Tokyo: Kasama shoin.
Kornicki, Peter F. 2018. *Languages, Scripts, and Chinese Texts in East Asia*. Oxford: Oxford University Press.
Levy, Indra A., ed. 2011. *Translation in Modern Japan* (Routledge Contemporary Japan Series). Abingdon: Routledge.
Lillis, Theresa M. 2013. *The Sociolinguistics of Writing*. Edinburgh: Edinburgh University Press.
Liu Lydia He. 1995. *Translingual Practice: Literature, National Culture, and Translated Modernity: China, 1900–1937*. Stanford, CA: Stanford University Press.
Lurie, David Barnett. 2011. *Realms of Literacy: Early Japan and the History of Writing* (Harvard East Asian Monographs 335). Cambridge, MA: Harvard University Asia Center.
Minemura Fumito, ed. 1995. *Shin kokin wakashū* (Shinpen nihon koten bungaku zenshū 43). Tokyo: Shōgakukan.

Nakamura Shunsaku, ed. 2008. *Higashi Ajia kanbun sekai to nihongo – Kundoku ron: Sei*. Tokyo: Bensei shuppan.
Nakamura Shunsaku, ed. 2010. *Higashi Ajia kanbun sekai no keisei – Kundoku ron: Zoku*. Tokyo: Bensei shuppan.
Nakamura Shunsaku, ed. 2014. *Kundoku kara minaosu Higashi Ajia* (Higashi Ajia kaiiki ni kogidasu 5). Tokyo: Tōkyō daigaku shuppankai.
Nakamura Shunsaku. 2017. *Shisōshi no naka no Nihongo: kundoku, hon'yaku, kokugo*. Tokyo: Bensei shuppan.
Ōsone Shōsuke, Gotō Akio, and Kinpara Tadashi, eds. 1992. *Honchō monzui* (Shin nihon koten bungaku taikei 27). Tokyo: Iwanami shoten.
Ōta Tsugio. 1967. 'Shaku Shingyū to sono chosaku ni tsuite: tsuki, Shin gafu ryakui nishu no hon'in'. *Shidō bunko ronshū*, 225–343.
Ōta Tsugio. 1968. 'Shinpukuji-zō Shin gafu chū to Kamakura jidai no Bunshū juyō ni tsuite – tsuki, Shin gafu chū hon'in'. *Shidō bunko ronshū*, 323–436.
Ōta Tsugio, ed. 1993. *Nihon ni okeru juyō: inbun hen* (Haku kyoi kenkyū koza, v.3). Tokyo: Benseisha.
Ōta Tsugio, ed. 1994a. *Nihon ni okeru juyō: sanbun hen* (Haku kyoi kenkyū koza, v.4). Tokyo: Benseisha.
Ōta Tsugio, ed. 1994b. *Hakushi juyō o meguru shomondai* (Haku kyoi kenkyū koza, v.5). Tokyo: Benseisha.
Ōta Tsugio and Kobayashi Yoshinori, eds. 1982. *Kanda-bon Hakushi bunshū no kenkyū*. Tokyo: Benseisha.
Reynolds, Matthew. 2011. *The Poetry of Translation: From Chaucer & Petrarch to Homer & Logue*. Oxford: Oxford University Press.
Reynolds, Matthew. 2016. *Translation: A Very Short Introduction*. Oxford: Oxford University Press.
Rodd, Laurel Rasplica. 2015. *Shinkokinshū: New Collection of Poems Ancient and Modern*. Leiden: Brill.
Saitō Mareshi. 2014. *Kanji sekai no chihei: watashitachi ni totte moji to wa nani ka* (Shinchō sensho). Tokyo: Shinchōsha.
Sakaki Atsuko. 2006. *Obsessions with the Sino-Japanese Polarity in Japanese Literature*. Honolulu: University of Hawai'i Press.
Shinpen Kokka Taikan. Electronic Resource (JapanKnowledge), https://japanknowledge.com/en/contents/kokkataikan/index.html. [Accessed July 2018]. Kadokawa.
Shirane Haruo. 2014. 'Mediating the Literary Classics: Commentary and Translation in Premodern Japan'. In *Rethinking East Asian Languages, Vernaculars, and Literacies, 1000–1919*, ed. Benjamin Elman. Leiden: Brill.
Shizunaga Takeshi. 2010. *Kanseki denrai: Haku Rakuten no shiika to Nihon*. Tokyo: Bensei shuppan.
Smits, Ivo. 1997. 'Reading the New Ballads: Late Heian Kanshi Poets and Bo Juyi'. In *Wasser-Spuren: Festschrift Für Wolfram Naumann Zum 65*, ed. Stanca Scholz-Cionca. Wiesbaden: Otto Harrassowitz, 169–184.
Steininger, Brian. 2016. 'Li Jiao's Songs: Commentary-Based Reading and the Reception of Tang Poetry in Heian Japan'. *East Asian Publishing and Society* 6 (2): 103–129.
Steininger, Brian. 2017. *Chinese Literary Forms in Heian Japan: Poetics and Practice*. Cambridge, MA: Harvard University Asia Center.

Suzuki Toshiyuki. 2007. *Edo no dokushonetsu: jigaku suru dokusha to shoseki ryūtsū*. Tokyo: Heibonsha.

Tamagami Takuya, ed. 1968. *Ukifune; kagerō; tenarai; yume no ukihashi* (Genji monogatari hyōshaku 12). Tokyo: Kadokawa shoten.

Tsukishima Hiroshi. 1965. *Heian jidai no kanbun kundokugo ni tsukiteno kenkyū* (2nd ed.). Tokyo: Tōkyō daigaku shuppankai.

Venuti, Lawrence. 2008. *The Translator's Invisibility: A History of Translation*. London: Routledge.

Wakabayashi, Judy and Rita Kothari. 2009. *Decentering Translation Studies: India and Beyond* (Benjamins Translation Library 86). Amsterdam: John Benjamins Pub. Co.

Whitman, John. 2011. 'The Ubiquity of the Gloss'. *Scripta* 3 (June).

Whitman, John, Miyoung Oh, Jinho Park, Valerio Luigi Alberizzi, Masayuki Tsukimoto, Teiji Kosukegawa, and Tomokazu Takada. 2010. 'Toward an International Vocabulary for Research on Vernacular Readings of Chinese Texts (漢文訓讀 Hanwen Xundu)'. *Scripta* 2 (September).

Yamazaki Kyūsaku. 1843. *Wakan rōeishū: hiragana tsuki kōshaku iri (和漢朗詠集 – 平かな付講釈入)*. 2 vols. Edo: Okadaya kashichi.

Yip, Leo Shingchi. 2016. *China Reinterpreted: Staging the Other in Muromachi Noh Theater*. Lanham, MD: Lexington Books.

Yoda Tomiko. 2004. *Gender and National Literature: Heian Texts in the Constructions of Japanese Modernity*. Durham: Duke University Press.

Yuzawa Tadayuki. 2001. *Kodai Nihonjin to gaikokugo: Genji, Michizane, Ennin, tsūyaku, Bokkai, Daigakuryō* (Yūgaku sōsho 14). Tokyo: Bensei Shuppan.

Zádrapa, Lukás. 2011. *Word-Class Flexibility in Classical Chinese: Verbal and Adverbial Uses of Nouns*. Leiden: Brill.

Zhu Jincheng, ed. 1988. *Bai Juyi ji jian jiao* (Zhongguo Gudian Wenxue Congshu). Shanghai: Shanghai guji chubanshe.

3 Translating invisibility

The case of Korean-English literary translation

Jieun Kiaer[1]

One of the biggest hurdles that arises in Korean-English[2] (K-E) literary translations is to translate invisibles – forms and functions that do not exist in either the source texts (ST) and languages (SL) or in the target languages (TL). As addressed in the introduction of this book, Venuti (1995) discussed the notion of invisibility in another sense, in the context of the longstanding preference in the Anglophone world for the creation of fluent target texts, with no signs of intervention from the translator (who is expected to be invisible). Venuti criticised this trend of erasing all traces of foreignness as a form of ethnocentric violence, arguing that translators should deliberately foreignise their translations to balance this violence. Like Venuti, I think it is important to recognise the powerful role of the translator; in this chapter, I argue for the primacy of the translator's discretion. The translator should be considered the co-author of a new text, and the treatment of these invisible expressions is their personal prerogative.

Dealing with invisibility is a challenge that K-E translators face at every moment of the translation process, from a micro-level to a macro-level, because the two languages are linguistically quite different. Common nouns in English are presented with articles, and specifying numbers or gender for pronouns is compulsory; in Korean, articles don't exist, and expressing number and gender is not conventional. It isn't only at the word level; the two languages also differ in crucial ways at structural and pragmatic levels.

In Korean, overall contextually salient expressions are usually unsaid, whereas in English, core expressions, such as the subject and verb, will be present almost all of the time. However, in Korean, it is impossible to end an utterance or sentence without choosing a speech style which reflects how the speaker views his/her hearer. This is not, of course, the case in English.

In this chapter, I show how translators deal with the invisible in their translation, providing examples from the premodern to modern eras. In

Section 1, I provide a bird's-eye view on Korean in relation to English; in Section 2, I present a theoretical background for this study and discuss the role of translators as co-writers. In Section 3, I present a number of case studies on address/kinship terms (3.1), speech styles (3.2), and poetry in K-E translations (3.3). In Section 4, I conclude.

3.1. Bird's-eye view on Korean in relation to English

Context sensitivity

Korean is linguistically very different from English. Structurally, the word order in Korean is different from that of English. In Korean, the verb comes at the end, and the order of the other expressions in a sentence can be flexible. Moreover, whether an expression need even be said depends on the context. This context-dependence and free omission of expressions means that figuring out 'who' did 'what' is often one of the most difficult challenges for Korean into English translators.

Speaker-hearer sensitivity

Korean is a speaker-hearer sensitive language. In English, it is not necessary to know to whom one is speaking in order to form a pragmatically adequate utterance. You can say, 'It is raining', 'It is two o'clock', 'I need to eat', and so on in English without knowing anything about your hearer. This is not the case in languages like Korean. Without first figuring out the speaker-hearer relationship, one can't even say a simple Korean sentence. The following three sentences all mean 'Did (you/he/she/they – the person) come?' but (1) shows the speaker's formal, honouring attitude towards the person who came; (2) is used to show a less formal, yet polite attitude; and (3) is used to show intimacy and is used between friends or a by a senior to a junior. This shows that even translating a simple sentence like 'Did he come?' into Korean, translators have to consider relational and attitudinal dynamics along with other factors.[3]

1   오셨어요 *osyŏssŏyo*? [formal – from a junior to a senior]
2   왔어요 *wassŏyo*? [polite – from a junior to a senior]
3   왔니 *wanni*? [informal – from a senior to a junior or between friends]

Speech styles and the accompanying relational dynamics are hard to translate into English because English lacks systematic linguistic tools to express these. However, when translating English texts into Korean, the translators have to create speech styles suitable for each text. As we shall see in Section 2, how to present different expressive/nuance-related meanings is under the translator(s)'s discretion, but even so, sometimes the demand to make visible what is invisible or invisible what is visible comes from grammatical conventions of the target language. As we shall soon see in Section 3, speech styles in Korean are, for instance, sensitive to age, social class and interpersonal relations (e.g., intimacy and solidarity). Deciding the right style is a complex matter – though it has been greatly simplified in contemporary society, compared to premodern society. In particular, achieving the appropriate balance between reflecting the senior/junior relationship and encouraging solidarity is key to creating the emotional environment for the text.

Fine-grained emotions and interpersonal relations

In Korean, a key to understanding emotions and interpersonal relations is embedded in a cluster of ending particles that are mostly one or two syllables. Though they may be short and do not contribute to the truth-conditional meanings, these particles are crucial in terms of creating a fine-grained emotional and relational foundation for the texts (Kiaer 2017). Consider another set of examples.

4 아름다워라 *arŭmdawŏra* [dialogue style, strong exclamation]
5 아름답네 (ㅂ+네) *arŭmdamne* [monologue style, light exclamation]
6 아름다워요 *arŭmdawŏyo* [informal, polite]
7 아름답소 (ㅂ+소) *arŭmdapso* [volitional, masculine]

English translations of these utterances could all be 'It is beautiful'. However, in Korean, they can have different emotional and interpersonal meanings. In (4) 아름다워라, – 라(*-ra*) is an emphatic/poetic ending. It is used to express the speaker's statement in an exclamatory mood. The degree of emphasis expressed by – 라(*-ra*) is stronger than that of – 네(*-ne*) in 아름답네 in (5). 아름답네 in (5), by comparison, sounds as if it was used in monologue. 아름다워요 in (6) is used in dialogue where the speaker is being polite to the hearer. 아름답소 in (7) is used in dialogue. The use of 소 (*-so*) sounds a little archaic and is most likely a male speaker speaking to a female hearer; it also portrays an intimate relationship, albeit with some formal distance remaining. In English, most of the time, it is auxiliaries or words that build up emotional and relational foundations for the texts. Broadly speaking, one can say that the roles of auxiliaries can be taken up by a cluster of particles in Korean, although particles seem to project much more fine-grained emotions.

Categorical adaptation: translating gender and numbers

The default position in Korean is for gender and number to remain unspecified. The Korean pronoun referring to 'she' – 그녀 *kŭnyŏ* – was introduced in the late 1950s through the Japanese word 彼女 *kanojo*, which in turn was a translation from English. However, even now, 그녀 *kŭnyŏ* is used only in some translated texts or to put some emphasis on the feminine nature of the person under discussion. Hence, 'she' can't be treated automatically as 그녀 *kŭnyŏ*. However, K-E translators need to meticulously search for the gender, often unsaid and hence implicit in the ST (Kiaer 2017: 43). Sometimes this process can be based on common sense or social conventions. It is interesting to see that the antagonist's unknown gender is often fixed as male. For instance, in *The Hen Who Dreamed She Could Fly* (Hwang; Kim 2013), the antagonist weasel is referred to from the beginning as 'he'. It is only at the last minute when his identity as a mother is revealed that 'he' changes to 'she'.

> The weasel got up immediately. He approached her, growling, his eyes glinting with rage. The weasel was so thin, Sprout almost felt bad for him . . . Then she glimpsed his distended stomach and nipples. Oh! Sprout was stunned . . . The weasel was their mother! . . . 'Please be merciful', the weasel pleaded, her voice trembling.
>
> (Hwang; Kim 2013: 124–125)[4]

In Korean text, no gendered pronoun was used to this point. Hence, although it would still be a surprise to an extent contextually, there isn't as dramatic and explicit a change as shown in the English text. Translators sometimes make assumptions about the gender of characters on the basis of their job or position.

In addition, although there is a particle that represents plurality in Korean, it isn't equivalent to English plural-marking in that the plural particle, 들 *tŭl*, is used only when the speaker/author wants to wilfully express some unspecified multitude or several-ness (Kiaer 2014). Hence, K-E translators need to make a decision each time how to depict events, with singular or plural entities.

Similar problems are found in many so-called grammatical categories, where in English, the uses of tense, aspect and modality are automatically set regardless of the speaker and author's subjective decision, unlike in Korean (Kiaer 2014). There are other issues that arise in K-E translations because of linguistic differences between the two languages. For instance, the treatment of kinship and address terms, as well as speech styles, poses a big hurdle for K-E translators – these categories are much more fine-grained in Korean than in English. We shall return to this in Section 3.

Challenges in translating non-European languages into European languages

As addressed earlier, most translation theories are built on translation between European languages, with only a few exceptions, and do not discuss the aforementioned hurdles in dealing with invisibles resulting from radical differences within languages and cultures. However, this Eurocentric view on language and translation is seriously limited in explaining the translation of non-European literature and scholarship, especially when it comes to translating languages outside the Indo-European family that have radically different scripts and grammatical categories and are embedded in different writing traditions and cultures. This book shows that translation theory and practice need to go beyond European languages and encompass a wider range of literature and scholarship. In this chapter, I explore K-E translation as a case study to support this proposal. For detailed discussions on different issues that arise in lexical, structural, prosodic and stylistic dimensions of K-E translations, see Kiaer (2017).

Challenges of translating Korean literature

From the beginning of the twentieth century, Korea has translated countless Western sources, mainly from English into Korean. Translation from Korean to English, however, only began in earnest relatively recently (Kiaer 2017). With its starting point in the international success of Korean TV dramas and pop music, *Hallyu* has been an undeniable phenomenon for over twenty years. However, the worldwide interest in Korean culture it generated has been slow to influence the spread of Korean literature. The export of music and movies was more immediate and met with an eager fan base more directly, while literature struggled to connect with interested readers, due to a range of issues, including translation, visibility and marketing. This may be why the increasing interest in Korean literature is too quiet and dispersed to be called a 'literary Hallyu'. Nevertheless, there has been a steady rise in interest in Korean literature in recent years, as can be seen for example in the awarding of the Man Asian Literary Prize to *Please Look after Mother* by Shin Kyung-sook in 2011, and the Man Booker International Award to Han Kang's *The Vegetarian* in 2016. Interest in Korean literature has not, however, been limited to novels alone: Korean poetry is also making steady inroads in the English-speaking market, particularly in the United States. However, the many translations of Korean poetry, particularly in anthology form, available for the English market today can be read in the same way as English-language poems, which disguises the often difficult process of translating Korean texts into English.

3.2. Translators as co-writers: theoretical background

Translator(s) as TT co-author(s)

Catford (1965: 20) produces probably the most well-known definition of translation, as transforming text written in one language (Source Language, SL) into an equivalent text in a different language (Target Language, TL), while maintaining the meaning and functional roles of the original text. The successful translation is evaluated based on its being suitable in the target language – without losing what is said from the source language. The word *translation* comes from the participle *translatio* of the Latin verb *transferre*, which means to carry over. This etymology is indicative of the longstanding view that the process of translation involves carrying a core, unchanged message across the barrier of language and fails to recognise any creative input from the translator; the translator is expected to 'transfer' the message in a way that is faithful to the original text, while also palatable in the target language. In reality, however, this is no easy task. Key criteria to measure the suitability of the translation can be divided into two groups as follows. See Baker (2011) and Kiaer (2017).

a   Source Language friendly translation values: *accuracy, formal equivalence, semantic translation, literal translation, foreignisation, alienation*
b   Target Language friendly translation values: *naturalness, dynamic equivalence, communicative translation, free translation, domestication, naturalisation*

Most of the time, translators make a decision that combines the two sets of values. Yet, translators are often faced with choices that could sacrifice one or the other set of criteria. Among these, faithfulness is one of the key responsibilities put on translators' shoulders. Translators are often expected to be faithful to the original text, in the sense of adhering to a close word-for-word approach but also to adapt where necessary for the sake of comprehensibility for TT readers.[5]

Translators, however, particularly in dealing with invisibles, face pressures from two directions: the SL/ST and TL/TT audiences. The SL audience is often enraged when the translators 'naturalize' or simplify culture-specific expressions and replace them with more accessible terms for the target language audience, accusing the translation of inaccuracy. At the same time, if the translators are too SL-oriented, the translated work will often fail to gain attraction with TL readers. Despite the creativity required to deliver a successful literary translation, the credit for such success usually goes to the author of the original text. The translator will, however, often receive the blame when the work causes a problem or misunderstanding in the target society and culture.

In this tug-of-war, translators have to mediate the languages and cultures of both sides seamlessly, from a position that is often marginalised. Venuti highlighted the overwhelming preference, at least in the Anglophone world, for translators to remain invisible, unheard and forgotten. They are often regarded as merely communicating someone else's voice. Yet, are their roles really marginal? Do translators merely speak with another's voice? Are they mere representations of somebody else – or even a subordinate to the author of the original text?

In this chapter, on the contrary, based on expressive semantics (2005), systematic functional grammar (Halliday and Mathiessen 1999/2004/2014) and my previous work on particles (Kiaer 2014), I argue that translators should be seen as co-authors of their TTs, alongside the ST authors. Through case studies in Section 3, I aim to show translators' authorship through the ways in which they create interpersonal and emotional meanings.

Relation between source text and (translated) target text

Walter Benjamin (1968) viewed translation as an 'afterlife' of the original work.[6] Though maybe similar, I want to consider the relationship between the Source Text and its translated Target Text as being closer to a sibling relationship than an afterlife. This is because often nowadays the translated text does not live after the original text in a chronological sense. Given the speed of some translations in the modern world, in particular of commercial successes like the Harry Potter series or books by Haruki Murakami, translations will often emerge very shortly after publication of the original. Han Kang's Korean novel *Ch'aeshikchuŭija* (The Vegetarian) came into life in 2007, and Deborah Smith's translation of this work *The Vegetarian* was published in 2015. Interestingly, the English version of *The Vegetarian* made *Ch'aeshikchuŭija* much more visible among Korean readers since Han and Smith received the Man Booker Prize. This shows one aspect of how the two – original writing and translated work – dynamically interact and influence each other.

The ST and the TT share a skeleton of meanings. In some cases, they may share a lot, but in another cases, they may share little. Just as siblings share a biological foundation, the ST and the TT share a semantic foundation. Yet, just as some siblings are quite similar to each other, sometimes like twins – although not all siblings are like this – there is a great variation in terms of how much or how little the two share. It is for the TT author, the translator, to decide whether to make the TT like a twin with the ST or not. A certain foundation is given in the ST, yet how to build it up is in the TT writer's hands.

Dual identities

While considering the identity of a translated piece of work, I was intrigued by the identity of ourselves and our words. In Kiaer (2018), I argue that like people, words of the world are gaining multiple identities and citizenships. I introduce the term *translingual words* to explain the identity of words that live beyond boundaries of languages. In this chapter, I also argue that translated works should have dual identities – both in the source and target languages – and their life trajectories as such should be respected by both ST and TT readers. Consider translating hybrid words. In contemporary Korea, English words are forming a major source of the everyday lexicon. Those words are often Korean-born hybrid English words. There are words that have come from English but are used differently in Korean. How can we translate these words – if ever we are to translate them? Or should they be left just as they are in order to keep the spirit of the words in the local context? This is becoming a much more common and complex problem, as we are now living in a multilingual era, where languages interact in an unprecedented scope and speed.

Multilingualism in translation

Multilingualism is increasingly becoming a norm in our time. It is not surprising to see a literary text written in a multilingual setting by an author with a multilingual background. *Pachinko* (Min Jin Lee 2017) is a story of Korean migrants living in Japan in the early twentieth century. *Pachinko* was published in English first and then translated back into Korean. Linguistically, it is interesting because of the layers of its multilingual setting. The author is Korean-American. The story must have unfolded in a mixture of Korean and Japanese, but we hear it in English through a Korean-American author. She must have vividly heard the imaginary voices in Korean mixed with Japanese. But she anglicises them as if they are invisible and unheard. In its Korean translation, however, the translator, Mijeong Lee, made the invisible and unheard sounds in English all visible and audible.

Likewise, *Princess Bari* (Hwang; Kim-Russell Sora 2015) is set in London, but the protagonist, Bari, is from North Korea, and other main characters in the novel have Asian backgrounds too. In its original Korean text, Bari speaks in the North Korean dialect. Then, she travels to China and finally settles in the UK. She communicates with others with a different linguistic repertoire, as if she is speaking her own mother tongue wherever she is, whomever she speaks to, without any sense of linguistic difficulty or awkwardness – though she must have spoken in English when she settled in the UK, and it must have been not so easy to do so. In the original Korean text, Bari's relation with others becomes visible because of the author's choice of speech styles – though in one sense, this is what is imagined in the author's mind, as all the characters must have spoken in English. In the English translation, those styles and relations become largely invisible – though the uses of address terms can still show the relational dynamics.

Translators often pick up italicisation in their toolbox to make themselves visible. Kim-Russell, while translating this text into English, chose to italicise the text when Bari and others were speaking in their own languages rather than English – mostly in monologue. This is invisible in the original text. Consider:

> I ask the women, some in full *burqa* and others with only *hijabs* covering their hair:
> *Have you seen Ali? Ali? Who's Ali? Anyone here seen Ali?*
> (Hwang; Kim-Russell Sora 2015, p. 198)

As we shall return to in Section 3, multilingualism brings a new challenge in translation, which is often viewed as a straightforward one-directional process from one language to the other.

Multiple layers of meanings: Potts (2005)

Meanings are like rainbows. This is because a rainbow is composed of many colours. The meanings of what has been said are also multidimensional like the colours of rainbows. For the last four decades since Grice (1975), semanticists and pragmatists have mainly been concerned with propositional meaning or truth-conditional meanings. However, Potts (2005) shed fresh light upon non-propositional meaning. Potts argued for the necessity of considering the non-propositional, expressive, dimensions of meaning and showed that there are two types of meaning, namely, (i) *at-issue* (inherently lexical) meaning and (ii) *commitment* (inherently pragmatic) meaning. In the tradition of contemporary semantic and pragmatic research, as Potts points out throughout his book, commitment meaning, which comprises an important part of Conventional Implicature, has been understudied or simply set aside as unimportant. Potts, however, proves that these kinds of meanings, often assumed to be peripheral, marginal or additional, are at the very centre of linguistic meaning. He also argues that sometimes commitment meanings – particularly those of expressives – are so powerful that speakers cannot use these expressions at all without wholly committing themselves to the expressive content. Consider (8) from Potts (2005):

8 That <u>bastard</u> Kresge is famous.
   a Descriptive meaning: 'Kresge is famous'.
   b Expressive meaning: 'Kresge is a {bastard/bad in the speaker's opinion}'.

The underlined expression *bastard* contributes to a dimension of meaning that is separate from the regular descriptive meaning. That is, no matter whether the propositional meaning of (8) is true or false, the expressive meaning projected by the word *bastard*, which reveals the speaker's attitude toward *Kresge*, is not affected at all. One of the main proposals of Potts (2005) is to show that 'commitment' meanings are as crucial as lexical meanings. It is almost impossible for us to utter anything immune to how we as speakers view the event. In exploring the meaning of natural language (particularly spoken language), it is not only impossible but also wrong to extract and study 'purely' lexical meaning alone, excluding the real-life dimensions of what constitutes meaning.

Speaker-commitment meaning not only provides an independent meaning to the whole proposition, but it also surpasses other meanings. For instance, if I say '*Amazingly, John gave all his money to a charity*', the whole proposition sits under the scope of amazement. Figure 3.1 presents the layers of meaning building on Potts's model.

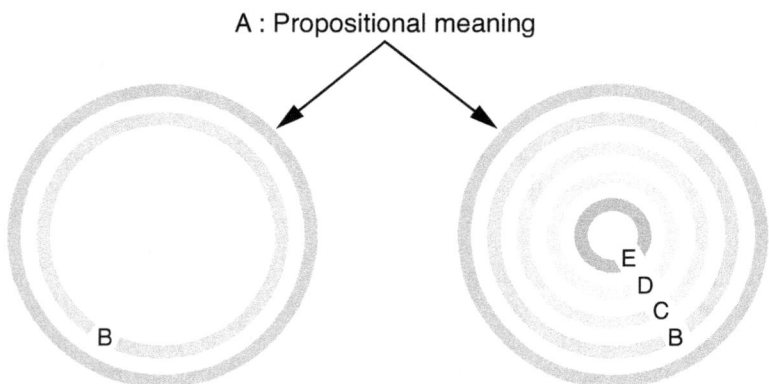

Figure 3.1 Layers of expressive meanings

Creating expressive meanings

Just as the expressive meaning described by Potts is not peripheral or marginal but one of the component meanings of an utterance, I argue that the meanings that are created by TT authors, the translators, are not marginal but simply form a dimension of complex meanings. TT authors start with the core meanings, inherited from or shared with the ST, which comprise both propositional and expressive meanings. Yet, translation is a creative activity, and fluidity is key. TT authors are free to pick, choose and reassemble meanings presented by the ST authors and create new meanings if needed and wanted. They can choose which meanings are to survive in the TT, the degree to which they are to survive, whether to translate or transliterate particular terms and so on as co-authors of the text in the new language and culture. It is worthwhile to mention that the copyright of the original text belongs to the ST author, but for the translated text, copyright is given to the translator(s) in most cases.

Take an example of translating swear words. Translators could just give up on word-by-word meaning altogether and find an expression that has the same expressive function. For instance, Han Smith (2015) translates 빌어먹을 *pirŏmŏgŭl* as 'Damn it'. 빌어먹을 literally means that the situation is so bad, and you are doomed to survive by borrowing food alone. This expression is used to express one's frustration.

In contrast, Ahn (2018) discusses translating 염병할 *yombyŏnghal* as 'May you contract the typhoid fever' instead of choosing the swear word *damn it*.

Translators' freedom

Translators have the right to re-adjust the works without feeling the need to follow the author's words meticulously. In this partnership, the ST author has to acknowledge and encourage his or her co-author's freedom to explore the texts in the new language and culture. Simply put, what has been said in the ST can be lost in the TT, and elements unspoken in the ST can be created in the TT under the new author's hands. It is the translator's freedom whether, and how, to translate these meanings. Consider the following extracted from Han Kang's novel 흰[7] *Hŭin* translated by Deborah Smith as *The White Book*:

> I spoke of my pet dog, who died when I was five years old. He was an unusually intelligent dog, I said, a mongrel, but descended in part from the famous Jindo breed.
>
> (Han Smith 2015: 20)[8]

In comparing Korean and English texts, the word 백구 *Paekku* 'white dog' is translated as 'pet dog' without the 'white' ness. The idea of a *mongrel* does not exist in the ST. The ST author also simply states that the dog is of the Jindo breed, but the translator added the word 'famous'. In addition, the ST states that the dog died when she was six years old, but the translator said it happened when she was five years old. The translator may have noticed the different age system used in Korea, in which one is described as already being one-year-old at birth and deliberately rendered the six years from the Korean as five years in the translation. Whether to literally translate six years old as being six years old or five years old – how much information to incorporate in translation – for the sake of the TT readers/audience – again depends on the translator, the TT author. The point I am making here is that neither the ST author nor ST readers should rely on a perceived requirement for literal faithfulness to the ST to condemn the TT author's decision to paint the picture in this way.

Translating subtle meanings

Expressive meanings that are lexically explicit, as in the case of *bastard* or *dear*, are less likely to cause any problems for translators. The real challenge for the Korean-into-English translators is to translate (almost) invisible expressions. As discussed, particles at the end of a sentence can project a complex emotional meaning.

In (9), the two sentences have the same propositional meanings and may be translated the same. But there is meaning difference caused by different particles at the end. 네 (*-ne*) could be used in monologue and shows light exclamation, whereas –구나 (*kuna*) is often used in dialogue where the speaker is senior to the junior, and it reveals greater exclamation in Korean.

9

예쁘[네]. *yeppŭ[ne]*.
It is pretty.
예쁘[구나]. *yeppŭ[kuna]*.
It is pretty.

Again, it is under the translator's discretion whether to translate such subtle meanings or not and if he or she does decide to translate them, how to do so. This is an area where TT author creativity can play an important role. This can be applied in both directions from Korean into English but also from English into Korean. As we shall see in Section 3.3, in translating sonnets, P'i Ch'ŏntŭk brought his full creativity to bear in making emotional meanings using particles in Korean.

Gradient model of translation

Suppose that the ST writer, known as the author, presented a set of meanings and the relationship among them. As said earlier, it is for the TT author (the translator) to decide how to pick out and reassemble those meanings and their internal relations.

Based on my observations described so far, I present a gradient model of translation in Figure 3.2. I argue that it is totally under the translator's discretion how and how much to juggle or negotiate the languages and cultures of ST and TT – though the two must share a kernel of core propositional meanings. In other words, decisions as to the degree of domestication or foreignisation are ultimately taken by the translator – despite the influence of external pressures. Though there is this freedom, *ethical* translators may not misuse this liberty and 'intentionally' distort the original meanings from the ST, observing that the ST text author too has the co-authorship for the text that he or she is creating. Historically, however, this is not unheard of. Ideology and censorship have often influenced translation processes (Tymoczko 2003).

In Figure 3.2, the author's meanings and the translator's meanings are not and cannot be the same – though some shared part is essential. The more they share, the more the translated work will be considered as relevant (Gutt 2000).

However, this is not the ultimate goal of translation. Fine-grained degree matters in translation. Translation is not a zero-sum game. There is great

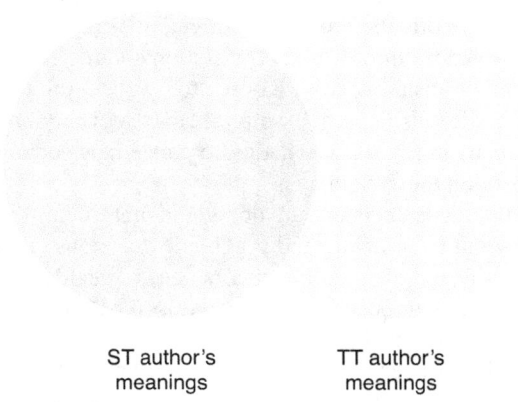

Figure 3.2 Author's meanings (ST author's meanings) and Translator's meanings (TT author's meanings): Gradient Model of Translation

scope for translators to bring their full creative force when it comes to expressive and attitudinal meanings; yet, when it comes to the propositional meanings, translators tend to show more faithfulness to the ST and its sociolinguistic setting, introducing less personal variations of their own. Of course, in translating non-existing categories, they will need to invent new categories. For instance, in translating words without any singular or plural morphemes, K-E translators need to create numbers relevant to the context.

Linguistic conventions

Though translators can have freedom to explore, there is linguistic pressure from the TL in translating invisibles. The pressure to follow the TL linguistic conventions is often far from the translator's personal decision. For instance, Korean-to-English translators have to specify the gender or number of the people under discussion. Likewise, interpersonal distance between interlocutors is often not clearly visible in English STs, but when creating a Korean TT, the translator has to establish a clear relational dynamic between the speakers in order to create meaningful and also grammatical utterances. Even if the translator himself or herself does not want to set any clear relational dynamic, he or she has to decide this, following grammatical conventions in Korean.

It is worthwhile to note that choosing a speech style is a linguistic requirement that the translator needs to accept in order to enable the translated piece to live in the written textual environment of Korean – although it is under the translator's discretion on which style to choose. One may decide not to choose a speech style in translation. For instance, in instant messaging, speech styles are often left unspecified. Yet, this could be experimental, and I have not seen any 'into' Korean translation conducted in this way.

Similarly, when translating from Korean to English, the translator must decide how to handle kinship terms, which are extremely common in Korean but lack equivalents in English – whether to create new social meanings in the TT or to abandon these elements.

Translators' linguistic decisions are not bound merely in word-level decisions but go beyond to syntactic and pragmatic decisions (Kiaer 2017). In providing a new life and identity, translators need to decide whether a word is to be translated at all or not. If they decide it is to be translated, they must decide then whether to transliterate or to translate.

Whether translators need to polish the language as well is another question. Is this included in the translator's job description? Particularly in poetry, there are many parts that sound ungrammatical and nonsensical. Then the question arises whether translators have to polish them and make them grammatical and sensical or leave them to feel the same.

Translating relations, attitudes and feelings: Halliday and Matthiessen 1999/2004/2014

Halliday and Matthiessen (1999/2004/2014) propose that language has ideational, textual and interpersonal functions. In particular, they stress the interpersonal functions of languages in that language is not something that exists in isolation: communication is a social endeavour.

Choice of words and grammatical structures is based on the person with whom you are speaking, the situation in which you are speaking and the result you wish to arise from the encounter. In addition, Halliday and Matthiessen propose the following as three components of register, which refers to the variety of language a speaker considers appropriate within a specific context to be composed of *mode, tenor* and *field*.

Simply put, the way we speak in a job interview will be different from the language we use with our children at the dinner table. Depending on the situation, speakers might vary their vocabulary, tone, prosody, style and so on.

According to Halliday and Matthiessen (1999/2004/2014), *Tenor* refers to 'the type of role interaction, the set of relevant social relations, permanent and temporary, among the participants involved'. Tenor is analysed from an interpersonal point of view and often involves a lot of 'reading between the lines'. It reveals information about what kind of person the author/speaker is (or is pretending to be), how strongly the author/speaker believes in the truth of the message, whether the author and the reader/listener are on equal terms or not and so on. Understanding tenor is important in setting the right tone for the text.

Our particular emphasis is on the tuning process of the tenor and mode of the text, which happen in the process of translation. In order to communicate socio-pragmatically one needs to fine-tune the tenor and mode of the text. This is often considered the most difficult aspect in translation. For instance, this challenge arises in Korean into English text translation because of the complexity of interpersonal aspects and the uses of related particles in Korean (see Section 3).

Individual style matters

Style matters particularly in literary translation. There isn't one way to translate. There are ways to evaluate translations using the criteria presented earlier, but it is ultimately the translators who make decisions according to their understanding of the factors around the texts. As recognised by Skopos theory, there is no single ideal translation in relation to a given ST – rather, the suitability of a translation is determined by the objectives of that particular translational act. A translator needs to make decisions that are sensitive to the translation goal, and a key consideration for any translation will be the appropriate register.

Eckert (2012) introduced the notion of the 'third wave' of sociolinguistic theory, in which speakers use various styles intelligently to place themselves where they want to be in the social landscape. Style in this sense not only refers to a certain mode of pronunciation or register of speech but also includes the choice of words. That is, individual speakers choose words – beyond nation-state language borders – to place themselves where they want to be in the social landscapes. We can also apply this notion of the third wave in the way each translator makes his or her own choice in the process of translation. One point to acknowledge here is that within SL or TL, different registers are increasing nowadays too – both online and offline. Intralinguistic translation therefore faces the same challenges as interlingual translation.

I claim that translators' creativity in building meanings for TTs reflects their cultural capital. According to Pierre Bourdieu (1986), cultural capital is cultural knowledge that serves as the currency that helps us navigate a culture and alters our experiences and the opportunities available to us. I argue that the translator's ability to creatively and relevantly establish meanings for TTs depends on the cultural capital he or she has.

Crowd-sourced translation: translation in social media

Techniques and trends in translation are greatly influenced by digital technology and the development of social media. Special interest groups found in online space add an important aspect to translation. For instance, Korean drama fans across the world add subtitles within a day from the first release of an episode, which are then viewed by a few million people. Most of these subtitlers are not professional translators but fans. These amateur translators, particularly translating into English, are growing in number as English becomes the lingua franca of our time. Those translators work through social media, and their impact and roles are not marginal. They make the translation process much more dynamic and interactive between source and target language audience.

For instance, the Korean word *oppa* in Korean drama is often transcribed as *oppa* instead of being translated as 'older brother'. This is a term used by a younger sister to refer to her older brother. Age and gender factors are engraved in the original Korean word *oppa*. This term can be used towards an older male who perhaps went to the same school or from the same hometown with the female speaker. Hence, in Korean, *oppa* is used exclusively by a younger female towards an older male. However, the word *oppa* has spread out through the Korean wave, and *oppa* in World Englishes nowadays means more or less 'a cool or hot guy' (Khedun-Burgoine 2018). It is worth noting that this changed meaning (lacking age-sensitivity) has started to influence the meaning of *oppa* in Korean texts (Kiaer 2018).

3.3. Case study

In this section, I present how K-E translators, TT authors, have dealt with challenges that arise through translating address terms and kinship terms (3.3.1.), speech styles (3.3.2.) and poetry (3.3.3.). What we witness is the increased stylistic variations accompanied by the complex life trajectories of the translators and their works.

Address terms and kinship terms

As discussed briefly in Section 1, in Korean, people do not call each other's names without proper kinship or address terms or vocative particles. For instance, one could address a person called *Jina* in the following ways.

> Jina-**ya** [shows intimacy, used when an adult calls out a child or used between friends with similar ages]
> Kim Jina-**ssi** [shows neutral respect and distance – it is still uncomfortable for a young person to call an older person with -ssi]
> Kim Jina-**nim** [shows more respect than -ssi]
> Jina-**yang** [mostly in a school context used by a teacher to call his or her female pupil]

Yet, if there is a job title, then that is used instead.

> Kim Jina **sŏnsaengnim** [teacher Kim Jina]
> Kim Jina **pujangnim** [director Kim Jina]

Choosing the right address terms is essential in communicating in Korean. Particularly, in premodern Korea, where a strict class system was used, the wrong or inappropriate uses of address terms was impossible and unforgivable. In premodern Korea, the uses of address terms show the social status of the speaker, hearer and the audience. In modern Korea, where the class system no longer exists, age became a more significant factor than the social hierarchy, and the address terms are largely simplified (Lee and Ramsey 2000).

Yet, even so, it is still a crucial matter to address people with an appropriate term. The wrong use of an address term can create conflicts in communication and damage relations. However, if one uses formal and polite address terms consistently, it is also regarded as an unfriendly, distancing gesture. The choice of the right address terms is indeed a complex matter. It can reflect social hierarchy and power but also at the same time can be used as a means to build solidarity.

Kinship terms

In Hwang Sok-yong's *Paritegi* (2007), Hwang uses *ŏnni*, *haraboji*, *ajumma* and *puin* in the Korean text to refer to the main characters around Bari. Kim-Russell translates them in English as, for example, 'Grandfather Abdul', 'Auntie Sarah', and 'Lady Emily'. It is interesting to see that Kim-Russell did not translate *Xiang ŏnni* in Korean as Sister Xiang. She left it as Xiang without *sister* or *nni*. In translating *The Vegetarian*, Smith translates *ŏnni* as 'sister', whilst in translating *The White Book*, she decides to transliterate it and chose *ŏnni* over sister. In *The Vegetarian*, Smith translates the two sisters again as 'sister' without mentioning who is older than the other.

> Sister, just behave, okay? Just eat what he gives you.
> 'Sister', Yeong-hye said, her voice low and calm as if intending to comfort her . . . 'Sister . . . all the trees of the world are like brothers and sisters'.
>
> (Han Smith 2015: 39, 144)

In the first example, the Korean term in the original text is *nuna*, as it is the protagonist's younger brother addressing his sister, while in the second example, the term in the original text is *ŏnni*, as it is the protagonist addressing her older sister. These distinctions are not transferred into the English TT.

Smith also uses terms like *sister-in-law* and *father-in-law* as address terms continuously. Again, seniority disappears through translation. In Korean, a term for your older sister's husband is different from that for your younger sister's husband. But that distinction is invisible in Han-Smith's translation.

> Sister-in-law, I asked, did you prepare all this food yourself?
> Sister-in-law . . .
> Yes.
>
> (Han Smith 2015: 35, 97)

In the first example, the Korean text refers specifically to an older sister-in-law. The Korean translated in the second example refers specifically to a younger sister-in-law.

Normally, age-related seniority is not translated into English as in the preceding example, but that is not always the case. *Kuunmong* (Nine-Cloud Dream), written by Kim Manjung (1637–1692), was translated by James S. Gale and published in 1922. This is one of the first novels translated from Korean into English. There, we can find examples where 'elder brother' is used as an address term.

> Elder brother, are you asleep? The Master is calling you.
>
> (Kim Gale 1922: 7)

In the English context, it would be odd to address old man living next door as *grandfather*. Using kinship terms like *sister-in-law*, *brother-in-law* or *father-in-law* as address terms could sound quite unnatural. Linguistically, English address terms are not as sensitive to age-related seniority. But, at the same time, first and second-generation Koreans often address others using address terms like those in the preceding example, even when speaking in English. While speaking in English, they feel bad and inappropriate if they address each other by first name alone. This is not only the case in Korean. This is the case in many Asian cultures. For instance, in India, one very common practice is calling older people you don't know 'Bhaiya', which in Hindi translates into elder brother, or 'Anna' in Tamil or 'Dada' in Bengali; both words mean 'elder brother'. For example, an elderly shopkeeper, a taxi driver, a fellow passenger or any bystander would be greeted as Bhaiya or Didi/Jiji (translates to elder sister) (Ayush Srivastava, personal communication). There is a strong tendency in Asian culture to establish a family-like relation with those who are close.

Using such address terms would cater to multilinguals particularly with Asian heritage living in an English-speaking world. In living English as a Lingua Franca (ELF) era, the notion of *foreignisation* is worthwhile to reconsider. The repeated uses of kinship and address terms may sound too foreign to those who are English monolinguals without any Asian cultural influence – but for those who have experienced Asian culture, this will not make them feel alienated.

As in all cultures, a difference exists between the address terms 'mom' and 'mother'. It is noticeable that in *Please Look after Mother*, throughout Shin Kyung-sook's Korean text, all her children and even her husband refer to her as 엄마 *ŏmma* (mum) rather than 어머니 *ŏmŏni* (mother). There is even a dispute found between the children on how to write a note on their missing mother.

> When you write, *please help us to find our mother*, he says it's too plain. When you write, *our mother is missing*, he says that *mother* is

too formal, and tells you to write *mum*. When you write, *Our mum is missing*, he decides it's too childish.

(Shin; Kim 2012: 5)

However, in English translation, *Mother* is used throughout with the first character M capitalised. There is more complexity in *The Story of Hong Gildong* by Minsoo Kang (2016), originally written by Heo Gyun (1569–1618)[9] when it comes to address terms in the premodern era. The main theme of the Hong Gildong [*Hong Kildong*[10]] story lies in the discrimination between children from a legal wife and concubine/consort. The protagonist, Gildong, cannot call his father *abŏji* 'Father' but has to call him *taegam*, which Kang translates as 'His Lordship'. In addition, he had to use honorifics towards his father's senior concubine Goksan [Koksan], who tried to kill him. In order to bring some distinction between the different concubines of Gildong's father, Kang 'invented' new terms, such as *senior concubine* and *junior concubine*. These are terms that literally do not exist in Korean yet were inserted creatively by the translator. Gildong, regardless of his personal position, because of Goksan's status being her father's concubine, has also to call her using a kinship or address term, which shows some – though not huge – respect and a close relationship. Kang hence translates the concubine as *Mother Goksan*, following its Korean word *koksan ŏmi* – where *ŏmi* in Korean here is used as a belittled term for a mother – normally used for people with a slightly lowly background in this historic context.

Ŏmi is less respectable than other terms referring to mother. But Kang translates *ŏmi* as *Mother*. It is probably not easy to find a term that could express a relation such as this. The decision to call his antagonist as *mother* was not made by Gildong's personal choice, but he did make the decision to submit sociolinguistic conventions of his time. In the novel, the senior minister's wife is also translated as 'mother' as in the following. Servants in Gildong's households all call the minister's legal wife as *mother* too.

> The assistant section chief sighed and consoled her. '<u>Mother</u>, please do not be so sad. We did what was necessary, so there is no use regretting it . . .'
> (Heo; Kang 2016: 15)

Mother here in the original Korean text is *manim*, which is used as an address term for the yangban's wife. As for royal wives, including the king's concubines, they are called by *mama*. Kang's choice of *mother* eliminates the distinction between the minister's legal wife and his concubines – at least in the level of address terms. I think *ma'am* could be also a suitable candidate in both cases because Koreans do not use the word *ŏmma* 'mother' when there is no blood relation. This is different from other kinship terms.

In *Princess Bari*, Kim-Russell translated *emi-ya* – the combined term of *emi* 'mother' plus *–ya* 'vocative particle' as 'Little mother'. *Emi* here is not intended to belittle motherhood but is used this time by a mother-in-law to call her daughter-in-law with affection. – *Ya* brings more affection as well as age-sensitive hierarchy too. Yet, in Kim-Russell's case, often vocative particles as this are lost in translation. This isn't the case at all times. The following is from the novel *Pachinko*. The author Lee uses *-ya* in her novel and introduces age-sensitive characteristics from Korean into English. It is a one-syllable word, but it has such power that it brings with it the hierarchical relation between the speaker and the person he or she is addressing. Moreover, it creates a kind of relation where the older person has moral responsibility over the younger person.

'Fatso-ya, don't touch that', said Gombo sternly.

(Lee 2017: 19)

One thing to note here is the dynamics of the address terms found particularly in Korean novels. The problem is that particular address terms are useful only between particular people in a particular setting. That said, when the speaker or the hearer changes or even their sociolinguistic register changes, the address terms change too, along with speech styles.

In *The Story of Hong Gildong* by Minsoo Kang (2016), the assassin who came to kill Gildong, when he encountered Gildong for the first time, uses lower address terms to Gildong. Yet when he realises Gildong's supernatural power, he lowers himself before Gildong, addressing himself as *soin* 'small person' and also changing speech styles into formal and honorific styles. These changes are invisible in English translation. But, in Kang's translation, he adopts a new term '*noble sir*', which doesn't exist in the ST in order to show the assassin's changed attitude towards Gildong.

I am not the only one guilty of this transgression against you since this whole plot was conceived by His Lordship's young lady Chorang . . . I beg you to forgive me, noble sir.

(Heo; Kang 2016: 18)

In the premodern Korean texts, there are two ways for one to refer to himself or herself: one is used in a relation when the speaker is senior to the audience and the other one is used within a relation when the hearer(s) are senior to the speaker. The word for the latter case starts with the syllable *so*, which means 'little'. They include *soin* 'small person', *soja* 'small son' and *sonyŏ* 'small daughter'. As in the following, in *Kuunmong*, the protagonist Sŏngjin always refers to himself as *soin* 'small person' when he speaks to his master.

Yet, when he is speaking to his wives, he never calls himself *soin* 'small person'. This distinction is left invisible in English.

> I have now been a disciple of the Master for ten years and more, and have never disobeyed any command.
>
> (Kim Gale 1922: 7)

In Chosŏn Korea, often the ideal husband and wife relationship is depicted as being when they treat each other as a guest. They had to use honorifics to each other. Particularly, a noble wife had to call her husband as Your Lordship. Minister Hong's wife in the *Story of Hong Gildong* calls her husband as *taegam*, which is translated as 'Your Lordship' by Kang, and Minister Hong calls his wife as *puin*, translated as 'Lady' by Kang. There is some change in the late Chosŏn Dynasty. Particularly among commoners, they could use intimate speech styles, and wives were allowed to call their husbands *nanggun*, 'dear husband'.

In court literature, the address terms become much more complex. For instance, in *Hanjungnok* by Hyegyŏnggung Hong-ssi (1735–1816), which was translated by JaHyun Kim Haboush as *The Memoirs of Lady Hyegyŏng*, Lady Hyegyŏng does not call her husband by his name because he is the Crown Prince. Later, she cannot call her son by name because of his becoming the king. Between people in the court, the address terms are determined by their different and diverse roles.

In translating, the terms that have been adopted are *His Highness*, *Her Majesty* and *My Lordship* along with a few more. When a royal person addresses his or her servants, Kim Haboush translates these terms of address by giving 'officer' followed by the servant's surname.

Translating the second person pronoun 'you' poses much trouble to both K-E and E-K translators. Often, even in spontaneous Korean speech, saying 'you' is avoided because of its complexity. In English-to-Korean translation, translators need to find a socio-pragmatically appropriate 'you' in order to make the texts adequate to Korean readers. For Korean-into-English translation, all different types of second-person pronouns in Korean emerge as *you*. In *Harry Potter*, translated by Hyewon Kim (1999), the translator made the second person pronoun visible all the time as in English. The translator used 너 (*nŏ*) 'you' when relatively similar-age children were calling others or adults were calling children yet 당신 (*tangshin*) 'you' when adults were calling the other adults. Yet, the use of 당신 (*tangshin*) 'you' can be sometimes viewed as negative. It is more neutral to avoid the use of the second-person pronoun in Korean.

English writers or K-E translators start to diversify the translating of *you* with some emotional epithets or suffixes. In *Pachinko*, Lee introduces how the address terms are used differently by Korean Japanese living in Japan. For instance, *yŏbo* – a term used often between a husband and a wife – is used as a derogatory term when used by the Japanese to call Koreans in 1920 Japan. Consider, in this, we also see that the Korean-born word used in Japanese, *yobo*, is pluralised according to English grammar.

> *Yobo*s eat dogs and now they're stealing the food of dogs!
> (Lee 2017: 33)

In the novel, there is dialogue among gang members who use a lot of slang and swear words.

> That Hirohito-***seki*** (*sic*.) took over our country, stole the best land, rice, fish and now our young people.
> (Lee 2017: 22)

The affix -*seki* [*saekki* in McC-R] literally means an offspring, but in Korean, it is often used as an epithet meaning something like 'son of bitch'. In most of Korean-to-English translation, those emotional epithets have been lost in translation. But it seems that in recent years, they have started entering into English texts as a transliterated form.

Translating speech styles

Translating speech styles is a complex matter. In English, speech styles are less sensitive to age, social status and interpersonal relations compared to Korean. In translating Korean to English, speech styles are inevitably simplified. But this may not necessarily be a bad experience. Lack of speech styles in one sense could be liberating of all hierarchical complexity that Korean readers have to endure.

In the Chosŏn period, speech styles in Korean were much more complex than they are now. For instance, in *Hanjungnok*, when the Lady Hyegyŏng's status changes from daughter to princess (wife of crown prince), her father changes speech styles to her to the formal/honorific and polite style. Likewise, when her son becomes a king, she starts to use an honorific style towards him. These changes and shifts that indicate changed relations often remain invisible when translated into English. The degrees of honorific language, such as that used by royal servants, are also invisible in English. The only elements that reveal these relational dynamics are address terms, as discussed earlier.

It is only after the 1905 Gabo reform that speech styles became simpler. Before this time, social class and norms mattered more than age or personal preference in terms of finding the right speech styles and address terms. With the dawn of modernisation, such rigid use of speech styles started to crumble rapidly. In modern Korea, age and psychological distance are what matters in terms of finding the right speech styles. Although there are some disputes, it is generally agreed that there are six speech styles in modern Korean (Yeon and Brown 2011: 17) as follows:

1 formal style / *hapsyoch'e*
2 polite style / *haeyoch'e*
3 semi-formal style / *ha'och'e*
4 familiar style / *hagech'e*
5 half-talk or intimate style / *panmal* / *haech'e*
6 plain style / *haerach'e*

Formal and polite speech styles are considered honorific and are prescriptively used with superiors, strangers and non-intimates. The semi-formal and familiar styles are used by older adults towards younger adults and have the nuance of authority and formality. Intimate and plain speech styles are seen as non-honorific styles and are to be used with intimates or subordinates in terms of age or rank (Yeon and Brown 2011: 171). Rather than using solely one speech style, Korean speakers tend to use either honorific formal and polite speech styles or non-honorific intimate and plain styles together. Changing between the styles conveys different nuances. The formal style is used more when addressing someone of high rank in a formal setting, whereas the polite form is used more frequently when talking to a non-intimate of similar age and rank (Yeon and Brown 2011: 174).

The six-style system is complex, but the actual usage of speech styles in modern Korean society is more simplistic. Lee and Ramsey explain that 'Today . . . when Koreans talk about speech styles, the most common . . . contrast is between *panmal*, "informal, intimate speech" and *contaysmal* [*chondaenmal*], which, roughly translated, means "polite speech"' (Lee and Ramsey 2000: 251). In this simplification of six systems into two, *panmal* refers to plain style and half-talk style, and *chondaenmal* refers to polite style and formal style. Usually the representative *chondaenmal* form is the polite style, also referred to as the *-yo* form. Thus, the informal half-talk (*panmal*) and polite *-yo* form 'have come to be the twin pillars of the speech-style system of modern Korean' (Lee and Ramsey 2000: 260).

In contemporary Korea, speech styles became much more simplified than they were in the premodern era, yet still it is not easy to find the register-sensitive speech style in translating Korean text into English. Speech style shift, or deciding when to use which speech style, is not as straightforward as the prescriptive descriptions in textbooks and is a complex matter even for native Korean speakers.

According to Yeon and Brown, in Korean honorifics, speakers must 'calculate [their] relationship with the person they are talking to' (Yeon and Brown 2011: 171). Lee and Ramsey (2000: 224) among others regard age and social hierarchy or rank as defining factors in this calculation. Other scholars agree that speech styles are a function of power. Yi Chŏngbok shows in his research that power is the 'primary factor' in determining speech style and that power in Korean society is 'represented by age, status, social class, etc.' (Yi Chŏngbok 2012: 272). This view is widely accepted by scholars. However, the actual usage of speech styles is much more complex than these descriptions might suggest and often contradicts views like Yi's.

Other researchers have gone to further lengths to prove the importance of intimacy as a function of the half-talk shift (shifting from a higher form to half-talk), showing how it is often more important than the power variable. Park (2017), for example, uses reality TV shows to show that shifting to half-talk is a way to establish an intimate relationship and particularly that the failure of couples to do so indicates a lack of closeness in their relationships. Kiaer et al. (2018) shows that even if there is a conflict between social hierarchy and age, that is, between a young boss and an old subordinate at work or a young senior and an old junior at university, the two parties prefer to use half-talk style to build a closer relationship.

The shifting of speech styles is a key to understanding subtle shifts in interpersonal relations. Yet, from a Korean into English translator's perspective, it is hard to accommodate such meaning shifts.

In Hwang Sok-yong's *Paritegi* (Princess Bari), we can read the depth of interpersonal relations straight in Korean. In (a) Bari's grandmother shows respect to his son – hence, she calls him *chane* 'you sir'. But at the same time, she is expressing her intimacy with her son by choosing an informal, half-talk speech style. However, in (b), the grandmother addresses her daughter-in-law as *emi-ya*, which is intimate. Then the grandmother uses the same informal, half-talk speech style in order to express their close relation. In (c), Bari's sister Sook addresses Bari as *chŏnyŏn*, which is the combination of 'that' and 'girl', which has a derogatory meaning. The derogatory nature is untranslated, but the informal speech is kept in the half-talk speech style.

a 자넨 대학 공부꺼지 하구 중국말 로씨아말 다 한다문서 딸아이 이름 하날 못지어? (Hwang Sok-yong 2007: 12)

'You mean to say you went to college and can speak Chinese and Russian, but you can't come up with a name for your baby girl'? (Hwang; Kim-Russell Sora 2015: 5) b 에미야, 저것두 이름을 져주어야 하지 않갔나? (Hwang Sok-yong 2007: 12)

    'Little Mother, maybe it's time we gave it a name'. (Hwang; Kim-Russell Sora 2015: 6)

c 저년 때문에 귀챦은 건 맨날 내 차지야. (Hwang Sok-yong 2007: 26)

    'I get stuck having to do everything because of *her*'. (Hwang; Kim-Russell Sora 2015: 18)

In Hwang's *Paritegi*, the protagonist Bari's dialogues with multinational characters are expressed with different speech styles. What is also interesting is that Bari – though she may not have had an opportunity to speak in South Korean, from the moment she left North Korea, she communicates with the other multilinguals she comes across in fluent South Korean, Seoul dialect. In the Korean text, with Xiang, Bari speaks with a half-talk style, and this shows that both Bari and Xiang are treating each other as intimate friends. However, when Bari speaks with her antagonists, she uses polite or distant speech styles.

In Yi Chong-jun's (1939–2008) *Nunkil* (Snowy Road), we can see examples of formality, distancing, affection and humbling in interpersonal relations through different speech styles. The character of the son uses formal speech with his mother and uses his linguistic choices as a means of distancing himself from his mother. By using formal speech, which is expressed through the formal polite verb endings, the son shows his distant and cold attitude towards his mother.

    '제가 무슨 더운 때 추운 때를 가려 살 여유나 있습니까'.
    Do I have the freedom to choose a good or bad time?
                                       (my own translation – formal ending)

In contrast, the mother character in *Nunkil* uses soft and affectionate language towards her son and also exhibits cultural characteristics of humbling and linguistic layering. The sheer number of expressive particles used in the mother's speech is immediately indicative of her depth of emotion towards her son and their situation.

    '이번에는 너 혼자도 아니고 . . . 하룻밤이나 차분히 좀 쉬어 가도록 하거라'.
    This time you didn't come alone . . . then what about staying another night to rest?
                                                  (my translation)

For instance, the mother does not forcefully say to her son to stay one more night but by using – 거(*kŏ*),

> she even softens her suggestion so that it may not sound too strong – though she really hopes that he will stay. So much of the emotional craftsmanship that went into the maternal character of this text is realised through the use of expressive particles which arouse deep sympathy from the reader. Whilst the characters' explicit words and actions are, for the most part, stilted and unharmonious, the way in which they communicate using various particles and different speech styles gives the reader a great insight into their feelings about one another, even before their story is told.

In *Please Look after Mother*, all the children speak to their old, missing mum using intimate, half-talk styles, and this is quite common in Korean. But in *The Vegetarian*, speech styles used between the protagonist and her mother and father, who both forced her to eat meat, show her distance with them and somewhat the resistance she expressed to them. That said, the protagonist Young-hye uses the polite speech style to her parents with the -yo (요) ending.

> '보고 있으려니 내 가슴이 터진다. 먹으라면 먹어!'
> My heart will pack in if this goes on any longer Eat!
> '저는, 고기를 안 먹어요'.
> Father, I don't eat meat.

One question we have is whether translators need to follow socio-political conventions of the source/departing culture while translating. In the following, we examine the Korean translation of *Harry Potter and the Philosopher's Stone*, translated into Korean by Hyewon Kim.

First of all, for Korean readers, it does not feel natural for Harry to address the much older Hagrid by his first name. Also, when defining friends in Korea, being of the same age matters a lot. E-K translators need to establish new relational dynamics between characters by considering their ages. Consider how Harry's aunt Petunia and uncle Vernon speak to each other using a semi-formal speech style, yet Petunia uses polite speech styles to her husband.

Husband-wife talk

Vernon: '페투니아, 당신 최근에 동생 소식 못 들었소?'
  ('Petunia, dear – you haven't heard from your sister lately, have you?')
Petunia: '아뇨 ... 왜요?' ('No ... Why?')

In Korea, culturally, wives tend to use polite forms to husbands even sometimes when wives are older than husbands – although this is changing in that nowadays young couples are more likely to use half-talk to each other. It is also likely that Koreans have different attitudes towards foreigners' use of Korean address terms and speech styles (Driggs 2018).

Age and social hierarchy matter in Korean. Whether K-E translators need to observe this and reflect this as closely as possible in English depends on the translator's discretion and freedom. Likewise, as age and social hierarchy do not matter too much in English, whether E-K translators then try to set up plausible social and interpersonal relations which could have been the case if set in Korea also depends on the translator's discretion and freedom. They can easily build up completely new interpersonal and socio-cultural meanings – though it is rare to find examples of this.

Observing encounters with strangers can be enlightening. In Korean, one can see how the strangers can settle as friends through the change of speech styles – dropping of the politeness particle *-yo*. This, however, is invisible in the case of English. Very often, once the relation is set, the same styles between characters are used regardless of the register and relationship changes. Translators hardly change the speech styles of characters even when their relations become close – even between lovers.

Translating poetry

Poetry translators

That the translator has a role as co-creator with the original author, rather than purely a subordinate, is manifested most clearly when one looks at the translation of poetry. The given or propositional meanings in the ST may be too small to provide much of a clue on how to compose a poem in the TL. This is particularly true with premodern-era East Asian poems written in Chinese characters, composed with one-syllable characters packed with meanings. Invisibles are common encounters too. For instance, it is hard to find a Korean poem which shows a clear set of subject and verb. Seemingly ungrammatical, unconventional lines are experimented with too. Even SL readers often struggle to resolve ambiguity in the ST, which one will never be able to resolve confidently. How then can we talk about their translations?

Forms and sounds have vast importance in translating poetry. If prose translators' contributions are concentrated in setting the right tone of the text, hence elaborating expressive meanings, poetry translators' contribution can be considered as working through every dimension of the text, which sometimes goes beyond textual information and extends into multimodal resources (Dicerto 2018). For instance, poetry is often presented with a painting in premodern East Asia. It is as important to understand the painting as the written text in understanding poetry. Sound matters a great deal too, as most poems can be sung. If the ST poems are sung, the TT authors may also wish to make it sung – though it may not be easy. Han Yumi and Hervé Péjaudier are well-known for translating Korean *p'ansori* into French Pansori and performing it (Han and Péjaudier 2011).

In early 1920s Korea, there was a growing genre of poetry known as *pŏnyŏkshi*, which means 'translated poems'. Kim Ŏk (1896–?), among others, started translating Western poems. They took great liberty in translating those poems in a way that fully naturalised them to Korean ears and with the full force of their own creativity. The famous poet Kim Sowŏl (1902–1934) was his disciple. Sowŏl, influenced by his teacher, in 1926, translated Du Fu's famous poem 春望 *Chunmang*, originally written in AD 757. In the following, I present Du Fu's original poem in classical Chinese and Sowŏl's translated poem along with my own English translation. The underlined parts are the bits which do not exist in their counterparts.

春望 'Missing spring' (Du Fu AD 757)

國破山河在
城春草木深
感時花濺淚
恨別鳥驚心
烽火連三月
<u>家書抵萬金</u>
白頭搔<u>更短</u>
渾欲不勝簪

Pom (Spring), Kim Sowŏl (1926)

이 나라 <u>나라는</u> 부서졌는데
This country – this country is broken
이산천<u>여태</u>산천<u>은</u>남아있더냐,
but its <u>mountains and rivers still remain,</u>
봄은 왔다 하<u>건만</u>
Spring has come, but
풀과 나무에 <u>뿐이어</u>
Only upon the grass and trees.
<u>오!서럽다 이를두고봄이냐</u>
How sad it is! Could one call it spring at all?
<u>치워라 꽃잎에도 눈물뿐 흩으며</u>

Take my tears and scatter them over the petals.
새 무리는 지저귀며 울지만
The flocks of birds are singing,
쉬어라 두근거리는 가슴아
Be still my beating heart.
못보느냐 벌겋게 솟구치는 봉숫불이
Can you not see the glowing fire?
끝끝내그무엇을태우려함이리오
Until the very last, what are you trying to burn?
그리워라내집은
I miss my home,
하늘밖에있으니
For it is beyond the heavens.
애닯다 긁어 쥐어 뜯어서
With deep sorrow I try to tear it to shreds,
다시금 짧아졌다고
Until it is getting short again,
다만 이 희끗희끗한 머리칼뿐
Yet with just these few white hairs,
이제는빗질할것도없구나
<u>I no longer have any hair to comb.</u>

The poem by Du Fu has been translated into Korean many times. The first translation was published in 1481, soon after Hanʼgŭl was invented and promulgated. Yet, Kim Sain (2013) praises Sowŏl's translation of Du Fu's poem, wondering whether Du Fu himself, if he were to come back to life, could reach the emotional climax which Sowŏl creates.

> Looking at this poem, I can see that Sowŏl did not just try to translate the literal meanings of the original poem. It seems that he has been putting on the soul of Du Fu or perhaps the soul of this poem and is expressing it into Korean. Perhaps I think even if Du Fu from Tang Dynasty may come back to life again and live in Sowŏl's time, it may not have been easy for him (Du Fu) to reach what Sowŏl achieved in his translated poem – the climax of sorrow and frustration.
>
> (Kim Sain 2013: 30)

Word-by-word comparison when translating poetry may not be so meaningful. Translators give new lives to a work with a new voice in a new language. In Du Fu's original poem, there is a character 淚, which refers to 'tears'. This one word has been translated in various ways in the translations. Sowŏl translated 淚 as 눈물뿐 훌으며 *nunmulppun hŭtʼŭmyŏ*. Roughly, this can be translated as 'scattering tears only', which sounds grammatically unnatural yet poetic. In Sowŏl's poem, he repeatedly uses endings such as – 냐 (-*nya*) or – 라 (-*ra*). In 남아있더냐 *namaittŏnya* and 봄이냐 *pominya*, – 냐 (*nya*) sounds regretful and seems to express the poet's bitter frustration. – 라 (-*ra*) in 치워라 *ch'iwŏra*, 쉬워라 *shwiŏra* is an ending often used to express strong command or exclamation. The translator poet ambiguously uses – 라 (-*ra*). Hence, it can express the extreme frustration that he is experiencing, yet it can also sound like he is commanding himself or others to take away tears and let the heart rest. Meanwhile, the words 치워라 *ch'iwŏra* and 쉬워라 *shwiŏra* are an addition by Sowŏl, and no direct equivalent exists in the Du Fu's poem.

One line from Du Fu's poem 家書抵萬金 means that 'my family's writings have the value of millions'. Sowŏl translated this as follows:

그리워라 내 집은
하늘 밖에 있으니
Missing my home
As it is outside the heaven

Perhaps, the two – the original work and the translated work – share an emotional backbone or DNA. Yet, the two are very different. This shows that the translated work is not and cannot be the replica of the original work, and translators cannot be parrots or puppets of the original authors. Translators bring new life into the work by creating a new poem which shares some kind of emotional DNA. It is not a question of copying the soul of the original, which is impossible, but sharing some part of it.

Exclamatory particles and poetry

There are dozens of exclamatory particles in Korean, which express different qualities of feelings; these are nonexistent in English. When it comes to translating poems from Korean into English, these aspects inevitably become unseen. However, if we translate English into Korean, the translator must set a tone that is suitable to the original poem, and this is done mostly by selecting expressive particles in Korean. For instance, one can make the poem sound formal and rigid by choosing more formal endings. This is not a marginal matter, because it completely changes the feeling or atmosphere of the poem.

The following are several examples of famous Korean poetry, with examples of the sentence ending particles to be found therein.

In *Hyangsu* (Thoughts of Home), by Chŏng Chiyŏng, many of the poem's stanzas end with the following line:

그 곳이 참하 꿈엔들 잊힐**리야**.
'How could I ever forget that place, even in my dreams?'[11]

The English translation simply looks like a question. However, the sentence ending particle here is –리야 (*riya*), which implies the ridiculousness of the idea that such a thing could ever happen. – 리야 (*riya*) also conveys the poet's heart longing for his home. It is worthwhile to note that this ending is used mainly in poetry and sounds a little ungrammatical when used in other registers.

In *Sŏshi* (Prologue) by Yun Tongju, the following lines are found:

모든 죽어 가는 것을 사랑해**야지**. (I must love all dying things.)
그리고 나한테 주어진 길을 (And the path given to me)
걸어 가**야겠다**. (is the one I must walk.)

The Korean endings – 야지 (*-yaji*) and – 야겠다 (*-yagetta*) reflect the fact that it is clearly part of a monologue or soliloquy and show determination to do something that sounds difficult or unappealing.

In the English version shown here, the emotional dynamic as such may be hard to search through.

Perhaps one of the more famous Korean poems is *Chindallaekkot* (Azalea Flowers) by Kim Sowŏl. In this poem, the author was creative in his endings. He used the ending – 오리다 (*-orida*), which is not used in spoken Korean and sounds very poetic. It feels like a promise. The English translation may not have the same feeling.

나 보기가 역겨워 (When you grow tired of me)
가실 때에는 (And leave)
말없이 고이 보내 드리**오리다**. (I will send you without a word, with grace.)

All of these examples of Korean poems include the sentence ending particles, which project attitudinal, expressive meanings that are hard to translate into English. This illustrates how a translator must take on the role of co-creator. Translation of Korean to English, as we have shown, requires that special care be taken with sentence ending particles. English to Korean translation also requires special focus on sentence ending particles. These particles, nonexistent in English, are essential to creating voice and emotion in Korean.

Shakespeare's sonnets have been translated many times by many different translators into Korean. Some translations of these sonnets are quite mechanical, capturing the semantic meaning of each line and transforming it into Korean. The following translation, by Pak Usu, is quite effective at expressing the meaning of the original. The first two lines of the poem Sonnet 18 are a good example of the type of translation portrayed here. In English, they read,

> Shall I compare thee to a summer's day?
> Thou art more lovely and more temperate:

This Korean translation reads:

> 그대를 내 여름날에 비할**까요**?
> 그대는 그보다 더 사랑스럽고 온유합**니다**.
> (Shakespeare Pak Usu 2011)

The sentence endings used here are interesting. The particles attached to the first verb are –까 (*kka*) and 요 (*yo*). This ending depicts the relation between the protagonist and his/her lover to be a polite-distant, respectful one. The next line ends with the word 온유하-(*onyuha-*), with the sentence ending –합니다 (*hamnida*), this time a formal ending, again expressing deference and distance.

Another translator, P'i Ch'ŏntŭk, took a different approach to the translation of this sonnet, translating the first two lines as follows:

> 내 그대를 한여름날에 비겨볼**까**?
> 그대는 더 아름답고 더 화창하여라.
> (Shakespeare P'i 2008)

The first line ends with the particle –까 (*kka*), which implies a feeling of soliloquy or intimacy, as compared with the conversational –까요 (*kkayo*) seen in the previous translation by Park. In P'i's translation, we can see that the relation between the protagonist and his or her lover is intimate and rather equal. It is noticeable that Park translates most of the sonnets in a conversational register, where the protagonist is talking as if his or her lover is present at the time of speaking the poem, whereas P'i translates most of the sonnets in a monologue or soliloquy tone, where the protagonist is more likely expressing his or her thoughts to him- or herself, and sets the lovers' relations as more intimate and equal.

3.4. Conclusion

In this chapter, I have discussed the issues that arise in translating invisibles in the case of Korean-English literary translation. The two languages are linguistically quite different, and a translator will frequently encounter invisibles. In this chapter, based on Potts's multi-modal, expressive semantics and

Halliday and Matthiessen's systematic functional linguistics, I propose the gradient model of translation and argue that translators are not subordinate to the ST authors but co-creators of the translated target texts. Simply speaking, translated work cannot be a replica of the original work. Translators' creative potential is most clearly visible in poetry translation (3.3). Translating speech styles (3.2) is challenging particularly in K-E translation because emotional dynamics are expressed by a set of particles in Korean, which have no place in English. How to establish the emotional, interpersonal environment using the given resources is then under the discretion of the translator. Translating speech styles is also a complex matter. In English, speech styles are less sensitive to age, social status and interpersonal relations than in Korean. In K-E translation, speech styles are inevitably simplified. But this is not necessarily a bad experience. The lack of speech styles might be liberating in the sense of removing much of the hierarchical complexity that Korean readers have to endure. Deciding the nature and degree of foreignisation in translation into English needs rethinking as we face the era of English as Lingua Franca (ELF). Particularly, kinship and address terms in Asian languages (3.1.), which were often left untranslated in the past, are becoming more visible nowadays either in translated or transliterated forms, and this, I think, can cater to English speakers with Asian heritage well.

Notes

1 I am grateful to Ben Cagan, Sophie Bowman, Anna Yates-Lu and Derek Driggs for their input and discussion.
2 I use K-E translations to refer to both from Korean-into-English and from English-into-Korean translations.
3 In this chapter, romanisations following the McCune-Reischauer system are provided alongside Korean words or short phrases. For longer sections of text, romanised transliterations are not provided.
4 In this chapter, citations for translated works are given with both the ST author and the translator's names (in that order).
5 There is another approach in translation called Skopos theory, where the suitability of a translation is determined by its Skopos (meaning goal) (Nord 2001). Skopos theory recognises translation as an 'act', which like all acts must have a goal. For example, a translation of Shakespeare's *Hamlet* into a Japanese manga comic with language easily understandable for children, maybe removing certain adult themes, could be considered a good translation if the goal is to give young Japanese children an introduction to Shakespeare, even if the product is completely different to the ST. Skopos theory is a bit of a shift because it challenges the primacy of equivalence. Even so, the Skopos, as determined by a translator's client, will often be to somehow faithfully translate the ST with as few interventions as possible (as if the very act of translation is not an intervention).
6 Caroline Disler (2011) recognises that the term 'afterlife' here is a translation, Walter Benjamin having written *Die Aufgabe des Übersetzers* in German, and questions whether Benjamin's original intention has been misinterpreted (perhaps

reinterpreted) as a result of the translation. It is interesting to find such a powerful example of the 'afterlife' of a text in translation in translations of this essay itself.
7 It is interesting to see that the original title in Korean is 흰, which means 'white' and has the feeling of incompleteness – waiting for a noun to modify to follow in Korean. The feelings of incompleteness however disappear in its English title *The White Book*.
8 In recognition of the concept that the translator is the author of the TT, references to translated texts in this book cite the translator's name.
9 While this is still the most dominant theory regarding the origins of *Hong Kildong*, Kang himself disputes this theory in the introduction to his translation.
10 Romanisation in this passage follows Kang, with the McCune-Reischauer romanisation provided in square brackets.
11 I am grateful to members who participated in the Korean poetry translation workshop in September 2017 to May 2018 at Oxford. Most of the translation presented in this chapter was done in collaboration with the poetry translation working group.

Source text list

홍길동전
Kang Minsoo. 2016. *The Story of Hong Gildong* (Penguin Classics). London: Penguin Books.

한중록
Hyegyŏng, Haboush, Jahyun K. 2013. *The Memoirs of Lady Hyegyŏng: The Autobiographical Writings of a Crown Princess of Eighteenth-Century Korea*. Berkeley: University of California Press.

마당을 나온 암탉
Hwang, Kim, Chi-young. 2013. *The Hen Who Dreamed She Could Fly: A Novel*. New York: Penguin Books.
Hwang Sun-mi. 2000. *Madangŭl Naon Amt'alk*. Paju: Sakyejul.

엄마를 부탁해
Shin, Kim, Chi-young. 2012. *Please Look after Mom: A Novel*. New York: Random House.
Shin Kyungsook. 2008. *Ŏmma-rŭl put'akhae*. Seoul: Changbi Publishers.

채식주의자
Han Kang. 2007. *Ch'aeshikchuŭija* (The Vegetarian). Seoul: Changbi Publishers.
Han, Smith, Deborah. 2015. *The Vegetarian: A Novel*. London: Portobello Books.

구운몽
Hwang, Kim-Russell Sora. 2015. *Princess Bari*. Reading: Periscope.
Hwang Sok-yong. 2007. *Paritegi*. Seoul: Changbi Publishers.

Other

Lee Minjin. 2017. *Pachinko*. London: Apollo.
Rowling, Kim Hyewon. 1999. *Haeri p'ot'ŏ mabŏpsa-ŭi tol* (Harry Potter and the Philosopher's Stone). Seoul: Moonhak Soochup Publishing Co.
Shakespeare, Pak Usu. 2011. *Sonet'ŭ* (Sonnets). Seoul: Yŏllin ch'aektŭl.

Shakespeare, P'i Ch'ŏntŭk. 1996. *Syeiksŭp'iŏ sonet'ŭ shijip* (Shakespeaere's Sonnets). Seoul: Saemt'ŏ.

References

Ahn Jeonghyo. 2018. *On Becoming a Foreign Writer*. Talk on Translating Korean Novels, University of Oxford.
Baker, Mona. 2011. *In Other Words: A Course Book on Translation* (2nd ed.). London and New York, NY: Routledge.
Benjamin, Walter. 1968. 'The Task of the Translator' [first printed as introduction to a Baudelaire translation, 1923]. In *Illuminations*, trans. Harry Zohn; ed. & intro. Hannah Arendt. New York: Harcourt Brace Jovanovich, 1968, 69–82.
Benjamin, Walter, Marcus Bullock, Michael Jennings, Howard Eiland, and Gary Smith. 1996. *Selected Writings*. Cambridge, MA and London: Belknap Press of Harvard University Press.
Bourdieu, Pierre. 1986. 'The Forms of Capital'. In *Handbook of Theory and Research for the Sociology of Education*, ed. John G. Richardson. New York: Greenwood Publishing Group, 46–58.
Catford, John Cunnison. 1965. *A Linguistic Theory of Ttranslation: An Essay in Applied Linguistics* (Language and Language Learning). London: Oxford University Press.
Dicerto, Sara. 2018. *Multimodal Pragmatics: Building a New Model for Source Text Analysis*. PQDT-Global.
Disler, Caroline. 2011. 'Benjamin's "Afterlife": A Productive (?) Mistranslation in Memoriam Daniel Simeoni'. *TTR: Traduction, terminologie, rédaction* 24 (1): 183–221.
Driggs, Derek. 2018. *Half-Talk Shift, Address Terms and Their Implications for Learners of Korean as a Foreign Language*. Mst Thesis, University of Oxford.
Eckert, Penelope. 2012. 'Three Waves of Variation Study: The Emergence of Meaning in the Study of Sociolinguistic Variation'. *Annual Review of Anthropology* 41 (41): 87–100.
Grice, Herbert Paul. 1975. 'Logic and Conversation'. In *Studies in Syntax and Semantics III: Speech Acts*, ed. Peter Cole and Jerry Morgan. New York: Academic Press, 183–198.
Gutt, Ernst-August. 2000. *Translation and Relevance: Cognition and Context* (2nd ed.). Manchester: St. Jerome.
Halliday, Michael and Matthiessen, Christian. 2014. *Halliday's Introduction to Functional Grammar* (4th ed.). Abingdon: Routledge.
Khedun-Burgoine, Brittany. 2018. *The International Fandom and Fandom Lexicon: The Globalisation of Korean Words through Social Media*. Unpublished Mst Thesis, University of Oxford.
Kiaer, Jieun. 2014. *Pragmatic Syntax* (Bloomsbury Studies in Theoretical Linguistics). London: Bloomsbury.

Kiaer, Jieun. 2017. *The Routledge Course in Korean Translation* (1st ed.). Abingdon: Routledge.

Kiaer, Jieun. 2018. *Translingual Words*. Abingdon: Routledge.

Kiaer et al. 2018. *Half-talk shift in Korean*. Presented at the 2018 American Association of Teachers of Korean, University of Toronto.

Kim, Gale, James. 1922. *The Cloud Dream of Nine, a Korean Novel: A Story of the Times of the Tangs of China about 840 A.D.* London: Westminster Press.

Kim, Sowol. 1926. 'Chindallaekkot'. *Kaebyŏk* 25.

Kim, Sain. 2013. *Shirŭl ŏrumanjida* (Looking after Poetry). Seoul: Pi.

Lee Ipseoup and Robert Ramsey. 2000. *The Korean Language* (SUNY Series in Korean Studies). Albany: State University of New York Press.

Nord, Christiane. 2001. *Translating as a Purposeful Activity: Functionalist Approaches Explained*. Shanghai: Shanghai Foreign Language Education Press.

Park, Mee-jeong. 2017. Negotiating Solidarity and Politeness in Korean Interaction. *International Journal of Korean Language Education* 3 (1): 197–237 (201–240).

Potts, Christoper. 2005. *The Logic of Conventional Implicatures* (Oxford Linguistics). Oxford: Oxford University Press.

Tymoczko, Maria. 2003. 'Ideology and the Position of the Translator: In What Sense Is a Translator "in between"?'. In *Apropos of Ideology: Translation Studies on Ideology: Ideologies in Translation Studies*, ed. M. Calzada-Pérez. Manchester: St. Jerome, 181–201 (188–209).

Venuti, Laurene. 1995. *The Translator's Invisibility: A History of Translation* (2nd ed.). London: Routledge.

Yeon Jaehoon and Lucien Brown. 2011. *Korean: A Comprehensive Grammar* (Routledge Comprehensive Grammars). London: Routledge.

Yi Chŏngbok. 2012. *Han'gugŏ kyŏngŏpŏp-ŭi kunŭng-kwa sayong wŏlli* (Principles of the Function and Usage of Korean Honorifics). Seoul: Sotong.

Yumi Han and Hervé Péjaudier. 2011. 'L'"autre" texte: ni tout à fait le même, ni tout à fait un autre'. *Impressions d'Extrême-Orient*, (2). URL: http://journals.openedition.org/ideo/225

Index

adaptation 5–7, 40, 49, 58, 62, 66–68, 72, 77, 84
allusion 24, 33, 35, 57, 65, 68
anonymity 7, 69, 70
at-issue meaning, commitment meaning 89, 90
authorship: co-writing 93; questions of; translational 69, 87

Bai Juyi 51, 52, 55, 58–60, 62, 64–66, 68, 69, 71–74, 76, 77

Chang hen ge ('Song of Lasting Sorrow') 52
Chen, Guying 16, 20
Chinese commentarial tradition 15; Chinese terms for commentary 35; interlinear commentary 35; similarities and differences between commentary and translation 4, 34, 41
classical Chinese: difference from modern Chinese 3, 4, 12, 13, 32; evolution of terms 11; as *lingua franca* 18; modern Chinese reception of classical Chinese literature 14, 33
colophons 69, 75
commentary 3–5, 8, 14, 16, 17, 20, 21, 34, 35, 38–42, 51, 52, 54, 55, 58, 69, 71–73, 75, 77

Daodejing 4, 14, 18, 19, 42, 43
Du Fu 109–111

Euro-centricism 85

faithfulness 86, 92, 94
Fang, Yong 20, 22, 25, 26, 28
foreignisation 10, 86, 93, 99, 114
formality 104, 106
format of text (ancient and modern) 26, 27; punctuation and the Chinese script 1, 14, 21, 22, 27
Fuboku Wakashō 66
Fujiwara Teika 64

gender 9, 81, 84, 94, 96
Genji monogatari (*The Tale of Genji*) 77
glosses: gloss-based translation 6, 64; paratextual glosses 68, 75
gradient model 10, 93–94, 114
Graham, Angus C. 18, 20, 23, 25, 28, 43
grammar: auxiliaries 83; mismatches 56, 70; particles 9, 59, 83, 87, 92, 95, 97, 101, 106, 107, 111–114
grammatical mismatches 56

Haku Rakuten 71
Harry Potter 87, 102, 107
Hen who dreamed she could fly, The 84
hiragana 52, 54, 55
Honchō monzui 63, 75, 76
honourifics: classical Japanese 64; Korean 105
hon'yaku 49, 50, 73–74
honzetsu (allusive variation) 65

intertextual sign/cue 62, 66
intra-linguistic/inter-lingual translation 5, 15, 42, 96

kanbun 49, 57
Kanda MS *Collected Works of Bai Juyi* 59
Kara monogatari (Tales of China) 66
katakana 59
Kim Sanghen
Ki no Tadana 63
kinship 9, 11, 82, 84, 94, 97–103
Kōzen, Hiroshi 20, 23, 28, 31
kundoku 5, 6, 14, 50, 51, 55, 57–62, 64, 65, 67, 70, 73–77

language contact: linguistic contact zones 50
Levi, Jean 18, 20, 23, 25, 28, 30
linguistic/conceptual evolution 27
linguistic conventions 9, 94, 100
Lingyuan qie ('The Lingyuan Lady') 58, 59, 61–68, 75, 76
Liou, Kia-Hway 18, 20, 23, 30
literacy: comparative study of 1; multiple practices of 8, 51, 52, 73
literary education 52
literary language 52
localisation 50

Mair, Victor 18, 20, 23, 28, 30
Memoirs of Lady Hyegyeong, The 102
Minamoto no Mitsuyuki 66
monzenyomi 57
multi-layered texts 72
multilingualism 1, 88–89

'National Studies Craze' 國學熱 16
numbers 10, 81, 84, 94

onyomi 50, 56

Penyeksi
Please look after mother 9, 85, 99, 107
poetry translation 114, 115
Princess Bari 88, 98, 101, 105
Princess Shokushi 65

recitation 33, 57, 60, 61, 69, 76
relational dynamics 82, 89, 94, 103, 107
relation between the premodern and modern 1, 11, 13
rōei 61, 75

Sanskrit 14, 26, 71
Shakespeare, William 112–114
sinology: sinologist translators 21
Skopos theory 95, 114
Snowy Road 106
social media/new media 96–97
speech styles 11, 81–84, 89, 94, 97, 101–108, 114

tenor 95
terms of address 102
three Realms 71
topic-line poems (kudaishi, kudai waka) 66
Tosa nikki (Tosa Diary) 70, 77
translation: collaborative 3, 50, 68, 72, 73; comparing translations 5, 19; cultural 50; differences between inter-East Asian translation and translating between East Asian and European languages 2; *Faux amis* 27; gloss-based 6, 57, 64, 73; *guwen jin yi* 古文今譯 (modern Chinese translations of classical Chinese texts) 4, 13; as interpretation 4, 6, 20, 23, 26, 28, 29, 39, 40, 51, 74; intralingual 3, 4, 11–13, 15, 32, 39, 42, 75; intralingual *vs.* interlingual translation 15; metaphors of 26, 55; paratextual 51; of poetry 114, 115; step-wise, distributed 69, 71; translating chapter titles and personal names 22–23; translating emotional nuance 31; translation across time 3, 13, 15, 33; translational fidelity 29, 31; translation and textual corruption 28; untranslatables 24, 26
translationese 51, 74
translingual practices 77
translingual words 88

Vegetarian, The 9, 85, 87, 98, 107
vernacular language 1, 3, 4, 7, 8, 33, 42, 49, 56, 58, 61, 68, 69, 73, 75–77
visibility/invisibility: linguistic 1, 4, 9; relating to reception and global awareness 19; translational 1, 2, 18, 31, 41

Wakan rōei kokujishō 52
Wakan rōeishū (Japanese and Chinese-Style Chanting Collection) 52; *hiragana tsuki kōshaku iri* 52
waka poetry 7, 8, 65–68, 71
Watson, Burton 18, 20, 21, 24, 25

Xin yuefu ('New Ballads') 52

Zhuangzi studies: different translations 15, 18–19; issues of authorship 16, 20, 42; *Zhuangzi* in East Asia and beyond 17, 18
Ziporyn, Brook 18, 20, 23, 25

For Product Safety Concerns and Information please contact our EU representative GPSR@taylorandfrancis.com
Taylor & Francis Verlag GmbH, Kaufingerstraße 24, 80331 München, Germany

www.ingramcontent.com/pod-product-compliance
Lightning Source LLC
Chambersburg PA
CBHW070739230426
43669CB00014B/2512